Land the Job

Six Months to Start Your Software
Career

Ryan Latta

Land the Job

Six Months to Start Your Software Career

Ryan Latta

ISBN 978-1-7344861-3-1

For my family, writing community, and the people who put their faith in me to help them with their career.

Contents

Introduction

Welcome to *Land the Job*! Before we get into the meat of the book, which will equip you to land that first and future job in the software industry, I thought I'd take the time to share why this book was written in the first place.

A few years ago I was working in a small consultancy, and we brought in a friend to join us. He didn't have any previous software experience, although we thought we could get him up to speed quickly. This began a two-year-long mentoring program between our new hire and me.

We covered all of the essentials needed to be a software developer. We taught what variables and functions are. We showed how to organize code. We demonstrated source control. What we taught grew in complexity as he learned on the job and from his mentors.

Eventually, he was ready to spread his wings and get out into the industry. He asked me for help in finding that first job, and our mentoring relationship changed. Over the coming months, I helped him develop his resume and sharpen his ability to find employment through scouring job postings and leveraging his network. We talked through how to get through the interviewing process and even salary negotiation.

After a few months, he landed his job. He got the salary of his dreams. My payment was a bottle of bourbon, and it was one of the best bourbons I've had.

I wondered if I could help someone else in the same way and I signed up to be a mentor again, this time with the focus on getting that first job in software. I suggested it would likely take six months to get that first job, and at the end of their six months they had their first signed offer.

While I wouldn't claim I have all the answers, I have developed a repeatable way to get a job in software. I honed this system through my career of ten years, and then taught others to do the same.

My goal is to equip people with the skills needed to get that first job and several afterward.

The Industry

If you look up the fastest growing industries, software development[1] has remained one of the most in-demand for years, and that trend isn't slowing down. If you keep looking, you'll find companies everywhere expressing the sentiment that they cannot find good people quickly enough.

You'll also find many people struggling to get jobs.

Companies are working hard to attract talent while simultaneously failing to hire it.

How can this be? Is the job that difficult?

Not really. My current hypothesis is that the software industry is so bad at finding people that it excludes perfectly qualified people because the candidates don't know how to navigate the hiring process.

I aim to equip everyone with what they need to be successful and maybe even prompt better hiring practices that render this book obsolete.

Beyond that, if we look at what it's like in software development compared to a lot of industries, you could do much worse. A given day for a developer will involve showing up to work in whatever clothes you're comfortable in at a time that is convenient. Your manager may show up at 8:30 AM, but developers might not show

---

[1]"Fastest Growing Occupations" bls.gov. https://www.bls.gov/ooh/fastest-growing.htm (accessed December 26, 2019)

up until 10 AM without any worry. You'll work at a computer that you've set up just for you. You can get some coffee and maybe a bite from the snacks that they provide. A few morning meetings with the team and you're into code. You can get up and take breaks with your colleagues. There will usually be an area to relax in, maybe play a game, have some drinks or snacks, and chat. The day ends, and everyone heads home.

The demand is high which means compensation is quite good considering the amount of training needed. The mobility of the workforce means that you will be able to search for increasingly better opportunities with little to no cost to you. This job can and will pay six figures—if you can get in.

There will be the other trappings that come with any job. Deadlines, poor communication, frustrating decisions, and so on is the stuff that makes any position feel like work. But you'll be paid well to get through those things, and there will always be another opportunity if it is too much to bear.

Software development isn't a job where you'll be at significant risk of physical injury. It isn't one where you'll be at high risk of being fired. It is a job that asks that you know the tools, techniques, and that you work well on a team. You can learn to do this job, and I can show you how to get it.

Thanks

Getting a job is hard work. I don't think enough people talk about how hard it is. My preferred phrase is "Soul-crushing." Applying for jobs and hearing nothing or hearing rejection over and over is tough to accept. I've often wondered if I wasn't good enough or if I wasn't cut-out for the industry.

I don't think that's true, but rather that the game is rigged. I believe at this point that getting a job is a unique set of skills that can be taught and learned. If you have the right skills for this maybe the search for that next job won't be soul-crushing.

There are so many things I'll cover in the book about the nature of getting a job in software that I don't want to spoil what is coming up in the chapters ahead, but I do want to make it a point to write this:

Thank you so very much. May you find a way to your job in the pages ahead.

1 - Land The Job

Land the Job exists to help you land that first job in software development. The information you'll find within the pages and chapters ahead are born out of hands-on practice from myself and from the people I've mentored over the past ten years.

Following the advice in this book has helped people get their first job in roughly six months and set them on a path to promotion and raises faster than they ever thought possible. When something goes wrong at the job, the information and skills you hone through practice will enable you to rebound into your next position.

Having said all of that, let's get into how this book is structured. *The Plan* will cover the broad plan that I've used for myself and with others to get a job effectively. Almost everyone should read that chapter so they understand the approach I'll further refine in future chapters. From there, each chapter explains in detail a specific element of the plan.

Resumes shows up early in the list of chapters for a reason. The chapter on resumes will break down the various kinds of resumes you could write and specific advice on how to write yours so that it leads to interviews. I will divulge how I created a resume with no experience that led to receiving a call nearly one hundred percent of the time. Resumes have that potential, so don't be in a hurry to skip through it. It is a foundational element to successful job searching.

Following resumes are *Cover Letters*. You may wonder if they're still relevant now, but they are. I've had interviews based solely on the strength of my cover letter. They are worth writing. We will consider the elements of cover letters and why they are so valuable. A little bit of warning, cover letters are less of a science than an art, but the payoff is well worth the invested time.

Up next are the other items to help you get to an interview. *Portfolios, Github, and Other Friends* will cover things like portfolios, GitHub, social media and conferences. You'll inevitably see a lot of talk around these things as being critical to the job hunt. I'll break down where you are likely to best spend your time in developing these aids and how to stand out with them. I'll also cover a topic very few people mention, which is speaking at conferences. If that's an avenue you're interested in I'll talk through how to get started speaking. It's an incredible way to establish yourself in a community.

Then we will get to looking for jobs. *Applying for Jobs* will cover things like how to read job descriptions. Reading job postings is a significant part of the process that improves with practical advice. I'll teach you what kinds of things to avoid in the job descriptions, what the words imply, and which phrases should deserve your attention. Also in this chapter, I'll talk through the importance of your network. I'll advise how to get your resume on the fast-track in a company by reaching out to people you know.

Following that, I'll talk about recruiters. They are an essential part of finding a position at many software development companies and are quite challenging to work with at the same time. My aim with this chapter is to prepare you for what you'll experience with recruiters and how to ensure that you are equipped to succeed with them. *Recruiters* comes at this point because everything covered so far will be described again under the lens of having a recruiter there in the process. It is that expansive.

After these chapters, we have the ingredients for a successful job search. The remaining chapters will take on the daunting task of getting you through the interviews successfully and ultimately to a position where you can get a better job or promoted quickly.

While interviews vary quite a bit, *Interviewing Strategy* covers the core ingredients that help you expertly navigate those interviews. I'll break the elements down and cover how to navigate each of the pieces the best way possible.

Next, I will describe the types of material you may need to know based on broad job categories, how to conduct yourself during a take-home assignment, and how to nail a whiteboarding interview. I'll guide you through some of the more unusual questions you may get asked that aren't technical but can lead to a strong impression. *The Interview Stages* is quite broad in scope but critical to the success of any jobseeker.

Probably the moment you are waiting for most is *The Offer and Negotiation*. After all the work and effort, you'll get an offer. It will be full of legal language and other things that may confuse you. Let me be the first to disclose that I am not a lawyer. There are important things to look for in an offer, however. You may decide that you want to negotiate those points and you may not, but you are going to be better off with the knowledge than not. I'll clarify those key elements to look for and what they mean, and where you may consider negotiating back.

Also, I'll introduce you to negotiation. For first-timers, I recommend reading that advice but not putting the advice into practice. For your second job on, it's worth bringing forward. Negotiation is a crucial aspect of getting the best compensation for you. I'll describe some of the key elements to setting yourself up to regularly get ten percent more salary.

How to use this book

With all this information available, where might you begin? Well as I mentioned before, I highly recommend you start with the *The Plan* where I outline the overall strategy I've developed. That will help give you context to the more specific advice found in later chapters.

Beyond that, you can use each chapter as an independent resource to help you develop the skill and excellence in each of those areas. You'll likely notice that the chapters progress in a way that mirrors the entire process. You may have questions about where things fit precisely, and I cover those in the topic-specific chapter and *The Plan*.

First Time

If this is your first ever software job, I'll recommend that you read the book until you finish the *Applying for Jobs* chapter. There will be a ton of material in there to digest. As you practice the content in those chapters and it becomes more comfortable, then start reading the chapters about interviewing.

The reason is that interviewing is a very different animal that comes with a lot of information to learn and a different set of skills. Trying to do it all at once will be overwhelming. Focus on creating interviews first, then focus on excelling at them.

After that, come back to chapters as you move through the process.

If you think you have the confidence to negotiate in your first interview, read *The Offer and Negotiating* before your very first interview. The words you use early in that process can completely change your odds.

Read *The Offer and Negotiating* about offer letters when you have one.

Second Job Onward

If this is your second or third job I'd recommend coming back to resumes again. Boring as it sounds, updating your resume with the experiences you've recently had provides an opportunity to distinguish yourself right out of the gate.

From there, I'd go back to the *Interviewing Strategy* and *The Interview Stages*. Look to see if there are questions there that you could do better answering. Look at how to whiteboard more effectively. Consider the stories you have ready.

Then look back at the *The Offer and Negotiating* on negotiation. As intimidating as it may be, the chapter on negotiation is written for the person that already has some experience under their belt and knows how to get a job. Maybe this is the opportunity for you to negotiate ten percent more.

Land the Job

What I'm about to write will be difficult or even absurd to read for a lot of people. That's because I'm going to detail what looking for a job is like in software. While most of what I write and describe may wind up being a fraction of what you experience, I've heard and experienced these stories enough that I feel obligated to share them.

The path ahead will be hard. I cannot overstate that enough. Finding a job is difficult and depressing. The process will likely leave you with deep concerns that you aren't good enough for the job.

That is untrue. You are good enough.

There are a few things I want to try to leave behind here at this moment. First, the hiring process for software developers is terrible. It is full of untrained people asking terrible questions that leave low confidence in the candidate they hire. Stick around and you'll find out.

Someday you'll get an email saying you need to interview someone.

More than likely you will feel completely unprepared to do the interview and you'll think back to all the interviews you've had and perpetuate some of the same things that you hated when you did this.

I say this to point out that most of the time we are interviewed by people who aren't prepared or trained to interview us. They will ask terrible questions. They'll give you terrible problems to solve. They may do things that are illegal and immoral.

This all happens more than you'd think.

This book equips you to get past all of this to the job that lies beyond the hiring foolishness.

For first-time hopefuls, the process will be especially hard on you. More than likely you will have an image in your head of what the job is like. It might be informed by friends or relatives. The truth is that very rarely does the hiring process reflect the job you'll be doing.

The questions they ask you during an interview will likely have no bearing on the job. The problem they ask you to solve will likely be done in a way that you'd never do professionally. They'll ask you for skills and experience they don't have. It is absurd, and it feels terrible in the moment trying to get through it.

So you are likely qualified to do the job, and the real question is: Do you know how to get hired? That's why you have this book.

I'd like to come back to a few things around the mostly broken interview process.

Soul-Crushing

Beginning with the premise that you are a person who has desirable skills and that companies want to pay you creates a conflict. The conflict arrives when a company decides *not* to pay you for the skills and knowledge you've developed.

This leaves many people wondering if they do have the skills or knowledge for the job. This seed of doubt that begins in the job hunt grows like a weed as many hopeful job-hunters try to get interviews and ultimately an offer. They reach out and hear nothing. They get an interview that they feel positive about, but it amounts to nothing.

When this is the experience in front of you, it is natural to have doubts.

My position on this is straightforward. You can be the best developer on the planet, but the hiring process won't bring that out. You won't be interviewed in a way that lets you show what you can actually do in the job. It will be full of tricks and traps that, if you fall into any one, will leave you without a job.

To get a job you'll have to steel yourself against the reality that the hiring process is not built to find out how much of a fit you are. It's built to find out how bad you might be.

As months go on in the search, what starts as doubt could blossom into the early signs of depression. Take how you feel seriously in this process. Self-care is a critical part of your career and begins in the search.

Imagine feeling like you don't amount to much and this whole search for a job is a waste of time. Then suddenly getting an offer. This emotional whiplash coming after the exhaustion that comes from feeling de-valued is taxing. Then you'll have to start a new job when you are giddy, yet exhausted.

Will you be at your best and brightest on those first days when you leave those first impressions? How easy will it be for you to absorb all of the information that is thrown at you when a few days ago this all felt pointless? Taking care of yourself is key to getting through the broken and painful hiring process and making sure you start your job off right.

If you realize you're not yourself in this process take this seriously and call someone you trust for help. Take care of yourself in this process and at all times. This is part of your career now.

Now that I've excited you with that proposition, allow me to tantalize you further with more specific examples of what the process is like and how it is built to prevent people from coming in instead of finding good people.

Information Asymmetry

Imagine playing a game of poker. Everyone is out of the game except you and your opponent. You each have your hands to play. If they win, you get nothing. If you win, you get paid.

You have one card in your hand. That card represents you. Your opponent has a lot more cards than you. Each of their cards represents key information that only they know that you cannot. They know the skills they want, the seniority, the pay, the benefits, the culture, the problems, the future direction, and so on.

To win at this game you will have to outplay them with your one card. The way you win the game is by making them believe that your single card is the one they actually need. It's the one card that makes sense with the rest in their hand[2].

This is the nature of interviewing for a job.

The reality is, though, that they have all the information about hiring you and you have none. You really only know yourself and your past. They know every other variable.

The very nature of hiring is unfair because they have all the information to make a decision and you have to influence that with none of it.

[2]Beck,   Kent.   "The   Prisoner's   Salary   Dilemma",   Facebook.com.
https://www.facebook.com/notes/kent-beck/the-prisoners-salary-dilemma/1655799601119564/
(Accessed January 19, 2020)

Here's an example. At some point in every interview process you'll likely get asked for your desired or past salary. I have a whole lot to say about this, but for now, let's use this question to highlight the information gap.

The company knows the pay range for the job you're interviewing for. If you say a number lower than the range, they may believe you're not good enough. If you pick one too high, they can't afford you. If you guess in the range, you'll be in the running. Going further, are you in the running but at the high or low end of the range, they were willing to pay? Did you say a number that cost you ten thousand dollars a year? Only they know that.

It's possible throughout the process to say something like that and end your interview. Some areas are known and can be taught. Some will depend on the specific circumstances of the job. Either way, you'll never really know what criteria they use for hiring you.

Your job is to make them desire you.

Trends in Hiring

Over the years, many trends have emerged in screening candidates. While these fads come and go, more than likely there will be one in place when you are looking for a job.

A few years ago, there was a big push to investigate people's social media presence. If you had posted something that was out of the line of the company's values or was less than professional, you might have found yourself in a pile of candidates who didn't get a call.

The difficulty that leads to products and trends like this is that hiring people is hard and expensive. Many organizations will reach for any promise to make it cheaper and easier to find talent, even if there is no efficacy behind it.

Currently, numerous companies have touted that they apply artificial intelligence and machine learning to the hiring process to quickly screen candidates. The craze around what people are describing as artificial intelligence and then using it in hiring is predictable. It will likely pass within a few years, only to be replaced by another fad in solving the problems of recruitment.

I was reading an account the other day of a human resources department that invested in such a tool. When someone followed up on a referral and found their referral was rejected, they discovered that the software had screened their reference out. So they sat down with Human Resources and went through the questionnaire the tool used. Even the head of HR was identified as unfit for the position when the tool was used.

While these fads and trends are almost impossible to avoid, they have an impact on your job search. When puzzling moments come, when you are without explanation as to why a company passed on you, this is yet another variable to consider. Maybe a tool that is part of a trend in human resources screened you out. Perhaps nobody even had a chance to look at what you had to offer.

Self-Care

Getting a job is no easy task. It can be hard, stressful, and even depressing. The truth is, not everyone has given much thought as to how to go about self-care in any aspect of their life. So before we get into how to get a job in software, here's how you might make the beginnings of a self-care plan.

First, take about five minutes and think back from the moment you're in now to times when you felt the most satisfied, alive, or fulfilled. Don't hurry through this. Five minutes will feel like a long time. As moments come up, hold on to them. Remember the feeling you had at that moment. Note what events and circumstances led to that moment.

When that's finished, reflect on the moments you recalled. Take a few more minutes and write down the things that were true that allowed you to have satisfaction, life, and fulfillment. During this, you don't need to worry about being certain. Try to find the ingredients that led to those moments that created those feelings.

Now that you have a list of ingredients, write them down. Put them near where you'll be doing the majority of your job hunt. For the ingredients you have noticed, see if you can't find a smaller list of things you can do to get that ingredient. For example, if an ingredient was "Great food with friends," you might think to host a dinner, meet at a favorite restaurant, go to your friend's home who cooks. Give yourself options to get these ingredients.

If you have time, try them out. You may need to refine the list a little, but going into this process with options that help you remember satisfaction and fulfillment will help you through this process and beyond.

If what I've written above seems to be a bit too out-there for you, that's fine. I'll simply ask that you think of someone that you can talk through this stuff with. They may only be a person you call to report what you're trying to do in the process. They may give you advice. They may be someone you can call and say, "This is really hard," and they'll listen.

Now, with all of that behind us, it's time to dive into how to get that job.

2 - The Plan

Welcome to the first of many chapters that will outline a strategy and techniques that with practice will enable you to get a job in software development.

This chapter will go through the overall plan I developed years ago, continue to use, and have mentored others in as they've landed their first job in software. This plan is by no means easy and requires a lot of work. Each success builds on the previous one, getting you closer to that offer letter.

In the last chapter I wrote about the terrible nature of software interviews. This plan equips you to expertly navigate interviews so that even if the process exists to weed you out, you make it to the end of the maze everyone else was trapped in. I want to show you how to leave an impression, stand out, and convince everyone to say *Yes* to you.

Time to get started!

A Skill-Based Approach

I consider getting a job the application of a specific set of skills to a problem. Think of Liam Neeson in *Taken*, where he says on the phone that he has developed a very specific set of skills over twenty-five years. That's how I think of this.

Building a resume that gets phone calls is a skill. Reading job descriptions and applying for jobs is a skill, even if it isn't a very difficult one. Having interviews with Human Resources is a skill. Have you ever felt flummoxed when they said, "Tell me about a difficult situation and what you did about it?" Learning to answer specific technical questions is a skill, especially when you don't know the answer. Learning to whiteboard or do assignments are also skills. Learning to negotiate a salary is a skill.

These are all learnable, practicable skills. My approach in helping people get hired is to put them on the path of developing those skills through education and experimentation. You may get far by following my advice about writing a resume, but you'll perfect your resume by putting it into the market and getting phone calls. The same goes for every other skill. You'll hone them through experimenting and putting them into practice.

If you find that my specific advice isn't working, you can still apply the idea of experimenting to find a better approach! I'm not a scholar on this subject, I've just interviewed a lot over the past decade and helped people find success with the same approach.

From 10,000 Feet

If we imagine all of the steps it takes to get a job, and that each of those steps can only yield two possible outcomes, yes or no, then this plan exists to create more yes.

When someone in the Human Resources department reads your resume and sees your application, they will potentially put you in a pile to forward along to a hiring manager. This is an opportunity to get an easy yes. The hiring manager will look at the same packet of material and they may do some searching. Here, too, is another opportunity for a yes. By now there will be a phone call for an interview. As cursory as these calls are, it is an easy yes when you demonstrate you are a living person interested in interviewing. This continues on and on. Each step we are trying to create a yes. Each step we are avoiding the no.

Here are the basic steps of the plan, and I'll go into a little more detail for each one.

1. Develop a resume that gets interviews
2. Apply to three jobs a week
3. Build a portfolio or other secondary material
4. Practice technical interviewing skills
5. Begin interviewing

It may help to think of these steps as cycles; in a nutshell you'll progress through each of these steps, but you will never abandon them. Developing your resume is how you begin, and you'll continue to do this even after you get the job.

Each piece of this process also exists to allow for experimentation. A resume is a great example. Most people I've encountered have not really given their resume too much thought. What if your resume was so refined that it would get you a phone call with almost perfect certainty? Wouldn't that lead to some form of experimentation as you refine your own? My plan encourages this and I will give you specific advice to guide your own refinement.

Your resume can do that.

The nature of experimentation is near-synonymous with practice for the intent of this book. It may not be obvious yet, but you'll be doing these steps dozens or hundreds of times. Getting a job is a whole skillset that requires practice and experimentation. This plan will require that of you. As I go into more detail as to the steps you'll see what I mean.

You may notice that my plan doesn't exactly line up with the chapters of this book. That is because this plan is your method, and the chapters are the specific guidance for each piece of the process during that method. *Portfolio, Github, and Other Friends*, for example, exists to help you develop a great portfolio and secondary presence for your job. Doing that exists within this plan that I've outlined. So think of the chapters as guidance for each of the pieces and milestones along the way. Executing the plan will put that advice into action.

Before I get into those specific steps I want to reiterate a point about all of this. I've mentioned practice, experiments, and skills several times now, and beneath all of the techniques those three words are the essence of this plan. You will experiment with how you best succeed. You will practice each skill needed through repeatedly engaging with the hiring process. You will hone your skills as you attempt to get a job over and over.

Develop Your Resume to Get Interviews

This first step of the process I really do owe to *What Color is Your Parachute*[3] by Richard N. Bolles. That book outlined what I have used throughout my career to build resumes that get me interviews. It is a wonderful book on the nature of securing interviews. My plan will go over the very specific advice you'll need that was inspired by Bolles and developed through practice.

As for developing a resume, the basic idea is that once you're equipped with the knowledge of writing a resume you'll take a stab at updating it. This we will consider your prototype resume. In other words, it is your first guess at a resume that will get you an interview.

Before moving forward, you may be a bit skeptical about how relevant a resume is compared to things like a LinkedIn profile or a portfolio or learning some new technology. In the current climate, you will have to give a resume for every position you are interested in. Even if you're a sure thing by all accounts, why invite any doubt with a terrible resume?

People use your resume to decide within sixty seconds if they'll spend even one more second on you.

---

[3]Bolles, Richard N. (2019). What Color is Your Parachute? New York, NY: Ten Speed Press

After you build your prototype resume you'll continue to refine it. You'll perfect it throughout the future steps and maintain it with your career.

This means you'll adjust your resume as you apply for jobs. You'll look over it again for how you can improve it across the board. You'll want to see how you can make small adjustments that make you a better fit based on the job you want. Build your prototype resume and experiment with it as you apply for jobs. Use the application process as a playground to experiment and tweak.

Then based on the interviews you get, you'll know that some of the changes worked and some didn't.

I recommend keeping a record of the jobs you applied to and the date you made your submission. That plays a role in a few other parts of the plan, but in terms of adjusting your resume you'll have a better idea of how to connect certain changes you made back to interviews.

Here's an example to get you started:

Company	Role	Date Applied	Interviewed On
Acme	Java Dev	1/23/2019	2/10/2019
Wiley	Jr Java	1/23/2019	

When I started off with no previous development experience, I couldn't get any interview calls. After going through this basic step intentionally I was getting nearly eighty percent success with my resume. I didn't lie—I learned to write a resume that put me in the interview pile. That's what this step is about.

Apply To Three Jobs A Week

Here is where the real work begins. Until interviews begin coming in and stacking up, apply to three jobs a week.

A very natural question would be *which jobs*? My advice is to apply for jobs you don't really care about. Certainly apply for ones in the field you are interested in, but don't worry if it's a company you like or if things look ideal.

Apply to three jobs a week.

The reason I recommend this is simple enough. Getting good at all of the things it takes to get a job benefits from practice. Applying to three jobs a week is the practice.

I wish I could say that you get the job you want by just sending out your resume and showing up. It doesn't work that way. Even a great company will have you go through an interview. Those interviews may be great or awful, but navigating them takes practice. Applying for jobs gives you that practice.

This approach raises some questions:

1. What if they want to hire me?
2. Why apply for a job I don't want?
3. Isn't this kind of rude or wrong?

What If They Want to Hire Me?

From the very beginning, that is entirely the point. You are doing this to get an offer. When offers start coming in, you can get a job where you want. The point is, you will be able to choose the company you want instead of the other way around.

Also—and this is very important—you are interviewing companies as much as they are interviewing you. Applying for a job does not obligate you to work there, just as the interview does not obligate the company to hire you. You are evaluating each other.

You will be walking into these interviews from the position that they will have to impress you instead of being desperate for a job. In terms of being in a healthy mental state to interview, knowing they need to win you over is far better than feeling like you need this particular job.

I recognize that turning down a job offer may sound insane, considering that the very nature of this book is to get you a job. The reality is that there are plenty of jobs and plenty of companies. Getting better at getting hired means you have choices. You can be discerning about the qualities of the company you want to work at. This freedom puts your career on a path of your choosing.

Seeing offers as choices and opportunities is the goal. When you're good at this to the point you get an offer, you can do it again. It's less about accepting the job you are offered and more about choosing the job you want.

Why Apply for a Job I Don't Want?

Imagine your dream job for a moment. Imagine applying with your resume as it stands and interviewing with them. What do you think the odds are of getting that job today? Now, imagine applying and interviewing to that same job after receiving multiple offers from multiple companies. How do those odds feel now?

Applying to jobs you don't want gives you the practice you need to get the job you do. Think of this as practice. Think of it as drills.

I want to be careful not to say that you get only one chance to apply to these positions. In my experience this isn't the case. Many companies, while they keep records of who applies to individual jobs, don't check for previous applications. So you can apply over and over. I wouldn't recommend applying in quick succession though.

As a counterpoint, I applied to three different positions at one company within a week. I got called for an interview within hours. I had to ask what position I'd interview for. And, by the way, I got that job.

So the intent is to apply to jobs to practice interviewing so that interviews aren't intimidating, so your resume is doing its job, and so that you know how to get them to say yes to you.

Isn't This Kind of Rude or Wrong?

For the final question about if doing this is rude or wrong. I'm not going to tell you how to feel about this, but I view employment at a company as fundamentally a business transaction. No matter what people say about joining a family or a culture or that I'm going to join something bigger than myself I'm always asked to sign on the dotted line. I will sign an employment offer, a series of contracts, and so on. In other words, all that nice-sounding stuff happens after our business transaction is complete.

That's a fairly wordy way of saying that I don't really have a problem doing this to companies. After all, even though my intent is to practice, I take every interview seriously. I'm open to the possibility that this opportunity and company may be a surprise I never saw coming.

I'll also point out that companies won't hesitate to have you spend weeks of your time and energy proving yourself to them when they absolutely will not tell you what they really want. They have no problem to request that you take a day off your current job to come in for hours of interviews. They see no issue having you work late nights trying to do an assignment they give. They are also fine not giving you an offer.

Here's another thought to consider. You'll find after being employed that some companies will often list positions, take resumes, schedule interviews, and put people through the process, even though they've already chosen who they want. They'll put everyone else through it so that the company can be seen as fair and equal.

Three Jobs a Week

Now, why three jobs? Well, it seems like an amount that is both challenging yet also doable within a week. Applying to jobs is a bit of a time commitment, but practically speaking in the beginning it might take about an hour per job. That means for the first few weeks you'll spend three hours of that week finding and applying to jobs. It's not massive, but it'll be a challenge.

Also, in the beginning, you need as much opportunity for feedback and practice as you can get, starting with honing your resume, but eventually learning how to nail those interviews. You need the pool of choices that come with applying for jobs. In the beginning it's pretty tough, but wait until you have multiple interviews for multiple jobs in a week. What a problem to have!

Build a Portfolio, GitHub, and more

This may be the most controversial thing I'll write about in this book. All over the internet you'll find advice about having a great portfolio, lots of GitHub activity, and an awesome LinkedIn profile. I believe these things are secondary in the process of securing a job.

Another way to think of them is that they complement everything else when done well. They sabotage you when done poorly.

To be clear, for first-time job-seekers these complementary materials may be exactly what you need to show off what you can do when you have no previous experience to back it up. After your first job, you'll notice that nobody cares. They care more about relevant experience than a beautiful portfolio page.

So then why do I put these last instead of front-loading them? I'm taking a stance. Every single job you'll ever apply to will require a resume—even the ones where you have a personal referral at a company. I emphasize the resume portion because it is required for every job and a poor resume will prevent your secondary materials from being seen at all. So I emphasize perfecting a resume first.

The other major factor here is that most of these secondary items take a lot of effort to do well. My advice is to delay these secondary materials, which take a long time to curate until your resume is ready.

They take a lot more effort than building a great resume.

Truthfully, you don't have to wait until your resume is absolutely perfect. If you think about what is most important then you'll be able to navigate the list. It doesn't mean that you can't start looking at building GitHub activity or a portfolio. It does mean that if you're more focused on those than on the number one priority—getting your resume to work for you—then you will flounder. Similarly if you decide not to apply for jobs while you work on these other things you've swapped priority and you will delay progress again.

The bottom line is you can juggle as many of these balls at a time as you'd like, but stay focused on the most important item every step of the way.

Another note about these secondary items, which reflects the bigger picture of what it is like to interview—when people are looking into who you are beyond a resume and into portfolios, GitHub, LinkedIn, or social media, you don't control what they see or think. If they find any one thing that they don't like, what will that do to your chances of getting the job if there is another candidate waiting?

I recommend putting this secondary information together as an attempt to create a narrative for them. Put these materials out strategically—in a way that gives you the best chance of earning a yes to the next step.

As a concrete example, if your portfolio site has even one JavaScript warning or error you have given someone who looks the opportunity to think that you are lazy, incompetent, or both. Even though in practice every website you've ever seen and even build for them will have warnings and errors, when interviewing you don't get the luxury of hoping they'll be kind.

These secondary materials are a great way of showing off what you can do but must be approached in a way that balances the effort with what impact they'll have on the people who see it. They must be built for the right audience and done in a way that invites as little doubt as possible.

The bottom line is that after your resume is getting you interviews, and after you are comfortable applying for jobs regularly, you have the foundation in place to enhance your chances by putting your best foot forward with these items.

I don't want to see people spending months building a portfolio site when their resume is so bad nobody calls them. Get the interviews running, then wow them with these other materials.

Practice the Technical Interviews and Begin Interviewing

This is the most daunting step by far. At this point in the process you'll be applying for jobs, getting interviews and then wondering why you aren't being hired, or more likely, feeling devastated after the experience and certain you won't get the job.

The reason to keep applying is to give you practice in this most crucial step. You cannot think your way through getting past these interviews. You have to do them. So now we begin to build the skills and disciplines needed to nail the technical interviews.

You'll discover that there are common technical questions that I call the *Gotchas*. The interviewer uses these questions to assess your capability by quickly testing if you know some tidbit. You'll find common ones through the process and learn to answer them. There are always more of these than you can learn entirely, but for any given job or tech stack you can find lists that will likely cover your bases.

When it comes to the parts of the interview where you'll have to show people that you can code there will be a different set of problems to solve and a different set of skills to learn. If you have an assignment, there are common trends that you can prepare for through small side projects. As an aside, these small side projects make good fodder for portfolios and GitHub projects. When it comes to whiteboarding, there are basics to know and prepare, and a skillset that allows you to succeed even if you can't solve the problem.

You may also get asked to pair-program as an interview, and this will be your best-case scenario even if it seems scary, because it will be the most faithful representation of you and the job you could hope for. Another viewpoint is that this will be the most straightforward and honest technical interviewing practice.

At this point you'll be learning how to navigate the dreaded technical interviews. This takes time and practice. Unlike the certainty I was able to offer about building a resume that gets interviews, I can give no such certainty here.

The truth is, I can't prepare you for every question you might be asked, and I can't tell you how to read an interview well enough to tell you that you've succeeded. The reality is that we don't know what they're really looking for, and so even a perfect interview may still not net the job.

In fact, one of my mentees interviewed for a mid-level development position. He nailed the interview, and friends that worked there said everyone loved him and thought he was great.

He didn't get the job.

What happened behind the scenes? A few days prior to his appointment, a senior person quit. When he interviewed they were actually seeing if he'd be a good fit for the senior role. He wasn't senior enough.

He also didn't apply for the job he didn't get.

There is a happy ending though, because they called him back after they filled the senior role and gave him the offer for the position he successfully interviewed in. That's when he found out what happened the first time around.

Bottom-line is that you can never know what is really going on when you're interviewing. You could be doing great, but for reasons you'll never know you don't get the job. So keep trying.

By the time you're getting comfortable with this step, it'll be time to start interviewing for the jobs you've had your eye on. It's impossible to know if you can interview perfectly, but if you're feeling comfortable with the process it's time to take the leap to get the offer for the job you want at the company you want.

Summary

By now hopefully it is obvious that there is a method to the approach that I've outlined. It is built around incrementally mastering each step of the interviewing process. The steps build on one another so that you get a higher chance of a *yes* out of each step, each success carrying you closer to the offer.

While they are somewhat sequential they can also be viewed as a priority list. If your heart is in starting your portfolio early, go ahead, but remember that without the other steps you may find yourself disqualified early in the process.

It might be helpful now to think about a timeline for each of these steps.

When it comes to building your resume, it takes a few days to create a prototype resume which you'll use from then on. As soon as the prototype is finished, you'll begin applying to three jobs a week until you get an offer. This step will last roughly six months. Secondary materials like portfolios, GitHub, and LinkedIn can begin at any point, but it's best to give them your attention after you're comfortable applying to jobs. Getting to this step may take a few weeks depending on discipline. Practicing technical interviewing steps will similarly layer on top of everything once the discipline of applying for jobs begins. The basics of whiteboarding and doing technical assignments are straightforward and benefit from mock interviews. Learning *Gotcha* questions can be taken on incrementally, a few per week.

With all these things happening simultaneously, it can be quite overwhelming, but in a given week you may find that applying for jobs takes less than two hours. Studying a few more questions takes another hour or two. You can sink another two-to-four hours a week into your secondary material, and if you're lucky you'll have an interview. This means that you can do this stuff for an hour each night and give it all the attention it needs. I'll leave that scheduling and rigor to you.

The next step of the plan is to learn the details of how to perfect each of the elements in the plan.

After finishing the next chapter, you're ready to start your six-month program to get the job.

3 - Resumes

Resumes are the currency primarily used in gaining interviews. It may seem old-fashioned, but as of 2020, this is still the case. Every company you apply to will ask you for a resume. Even if you have someone recommending you on the inside, you'll have to give your resume. If it's that ubiquitous, why take any chances with it? Make your resume a tool that gets you the interview.

When I started my career, I began by reading a book called, "What Color is Your Parachute?"[4] I used this book to develop my first resume and have since refined my process and taught others how to build resumes. This chapter is a dive into how to make a resume that leads to interviews—a resume that gets a yes in sixty seconds or less.

You may be wondering why I say sixty seconds? Well, if you're in the industry long enough, you'll start reading them too. You'll begin interviewing people after a few years. You'll find yourself on the other side of the table from a hopeful developer! After reading a few resumes, you'll notice that you can very quickly conclude whether you would be interested in speaking with them or not. Other people over the years have confirmed this experience. In some cases, it takes longer to print the resume for review than it does to review it.

The challenge behind a resume is to pique their interest in sixty seconds or less. To do this, know your audience and write compelling, outcome-oriented statements.

---

[4]Bolles, Richard N. (2019). What Color is Your Parachute? New York, NY: Ten Speed Press

No Lying

I'd be remiss if I didn't pause to say this is where ethics come into play. There are people who will happily lie to get a job. You may find that after reading this book, you'll know exactly how you could lie your way into a career. I suspect some people will do just that. Don't take this path.

The software development community is smaller than you'd think. After a few years in a market you'll wind up with a network of peers that connects you to almost every other developer and company in the area. If people find out you lied, it will follow you, and you will not be hired again.

What constitutes a lie? If you claim you worked at a place you never did, that is a lie. If you say you have a skill that you do not have, that is a lie. If you say you have an education you don't have, that is a lie. If you're using someone else's resume, that is a lie. I wish I didn't have to write this, and for most people, this paragraph will seem completely unnecessary.

I know from experience it is necessary. I've bumped into enough frauds over the years.

Myths

Now may be a good time to talk about some odd things you've heard about resumes. First, let's talk about resume length. You may have received advice that your resume has to be one page. You may have heard two pages. I've yet to meet anyone that discards resumes that are more than two pages, so length isn't your problem. The amount of time they'll read is. I am guilty of this. I sometimes receive resumes that are six-to-nine pages long. I'll have made a decision by the end of the second page.

The bottom line when it comes to length is not to worry about it. Do front-load your resume to have the highest impact as early as you can, but I have no reason to believe that length will work against you.

There are also some interesting bits of advice people give around making your resume stand out more—things like colored paper or artistic fonts, or other crazy stuff. Yes, there will be a chance that someone will be blown away by your creativity. Busy people, though, are more likely to find it jarring and irritating instead.

If you want to show your artistic side, *Cover Letters* and *Portfolios* are an excellent way to demonstrate creativity that is unlikely to turn people away from you prematurely.

There is a lot of advice out there about formatting your resume. As long as your resume falls into one of the three major kinds, you'll be just fine. I recommend a skills-based resume in this book, but I'll cover the others briefly. Here are some example formatting topics that seem not to matter when you focus on impact:

- Objective statements
- Career synopsis
- Correct number of bullets

Disqualified

Now that the myths are out of the way it is time to cover some ground rules. I don't recommend breaking these rules, as it comes with a higher chance of failure. The major things to watch for are:

- Spelling Mistakes
- Poor Readability
- Wrong Names
- Grammar Mistakes

Spelling Mistakes

If your resume has spelling mistakes, you're finished. That doesn't mean everyone will be scanning with an eye for typos, but if someone finds one, it will be brought up within the company. It may not disqualify you outright, but it will be a turn-off. Remember, resumes are still the primary currency in use for deciding to interview. Spelling errors are so egregious when spellcheck is electronically built into almost every tool on the planet. It shows an extreme lack of detail and general laziness.

Eliminating Spelling Mistakes

When it comes to catching typos there are a few things you can do:

- Have someone else read it
- Uncapitalize your entire resume
- Search for easy-to-mistake words like their and its
- Double-check spellings of specific technologies

Another set of eyes will assuredly find more typos than you reading it yourself. Get it in front of someone and ask, "Do you see any mistakes?"

Next, you can make sure no words in your resume are capitalized. Capitalized words are treated as proper nouns to most spell-checkers, and that means they'll skip them. So lower-case everything and your resume will light up. A lot of the new found things you will realize are fine. Consider adding them to the dictionary and fix it as you go. Uncapitalizing gives you a chance to catch mistakes with a wider net.

There are a few words that most of us mess up all the time. Search for them and see if you have the right one in the right place.

- Their/they're/there

- Its/it's
- Affect/effect

Last, for any key technologies and unique words you're using in your resume, take the time to double-check their spelling by going to the source, copying it, and pasting it back. Nothing stands out more than a typo in a core element of the tech-stack that you're interviewing for.

Poor Readability

If your resume is hard to read, you're finished. This advice mostly comes down to remembering that I as an interviewer will only give your resume sixty seconds. If you make that sixty seconds irritating due to formatting or a very difficult to understand style, I'd rather pick up another resume. Keep your resume format and design clean and consistent. Build it for the reader and not for your own sake of design. You'd be surprised how easy it is to see when things are inconsistent. It is off-putting and often begs the question, "How did they not notice and fix that?" As far as resume blunders go, it's right up there with spelling mistakes.

You can distinguish yourself easily by avoiding any spelling errors and having a clean, simple format.

As a small story, I recently worked with a manager who showed me how they read resumes. It was alarming. After they had done their sixty-second read, they would turn on the invisible formatting. They would make all the spaces, tabs, and returns appear. If they saw that sometimes you used space instead of a tab, you were finished. They wanted the resumes they saw to be crafted by someone who took the time to do it right even in the areas you cannot see.

Wrong Names

Here is another common and yet foolish mistake I see all the time: A resume with different names on it. This most commonly happens with agencies and consultancies, but it can happen as a first-time job-seeker too. It is very easy to start with someone else's template and forget to make that one last name change. Suddenly the resume has two names on it. If someone sees that, you're finished.

Grammar Mistakes

Lastly, keep an eye on your grammar and punctuation. They're not likely going to notice if you missed or added a comma in the wrong spot. However, they'll notice that some bullets have periods and some don't. They will notice sentences that run on or are incomplete. They'll notice the obvious grammar mistakes. If they find these mistakes, you're finished.

Audience

Knowing who reads your resume is critical in the process. Broadly, three distinct types of people will read your resume. Writing a resume that can appease each of them is challenging but very doable. The three major audiences are:

- Human Resources Professional
- Hiring Manager
- Peer Developer

Human Resources Professional

The Human Resources professional is the easiest to write for. They'll be involved throughout the interviewing process, but it'd be a mistake to assume they understand the job you're applying for. They have specific training and skills unrelated to software development. Yet they will read your resume first. How do you write for someone that doesn't know the job?

Well, the answer is in the job posting. The job posting was written by hiring managers and peer developers. It contains elements that the Human Resources professional can quickly scan to see if the candidate is a good fit. For example, if the HR professional knows that Java is a core skill, they can search your resume for the keyword Java. If it isn't there, they'll pass.

Writing for Human Resources is all about putting keywords in places that are highly prominent and searchable. You'll hone your ability to place keywords as you become proficient at reading job postings and writing resumes.

Hiring Manager

Next up is the hiring manager. This is your primary reader. They will decide whether to interview you in sixty seconds. The HR professional scanned your resume to ensure you have all the pieces there in terms of skills and claimed experience through keyword matching. The hiring manager will read your resume and weigh it against what they know they need.

For this person, writing your resume for impact and outcomes is key. This makes a very clear connection to how you work to achieve a goal. Almost every resume in the wild simply lists the duties and tasks performed. Yours will go further to say how you made a difference in those duties. You'll stand out. They'll want to ask, "How did you do that?" Writing to pique this person's curiosity is the real game.

We'll cover later how to adjust your resume for each job you apply to, but the hiring manager is your primary target. You can list skills you have that you know they need. You can adjust some of your experience statements to emphasize certain things you've learned by researching the company. For example, if the company is a consultancy or agency, maybe you want to emphasize how well you worked with clients or external people. This highlights a highly desirable competency that agencies and consultancies would almost rather have instead of technical prowess.

Peer Developer

Last on the list is the peer developer. These are your co-workers, though likely in a more senior position. They are unlikely to inform the decision to interview you or not. They will see your resume as they prepare interview questions. For this audience what you put in your resume in terms of skills and experience will lead them to ask questions more predictably. As an example, even though it had nothing to do with software development, I kept the fact that I lived abroad on my resume for years. It always garnered questions that allowed me to tell a series of stories that highlighted specific qualities, traits, and circumstances.

Pay attention to the things in your resume that consistently generate intrigue. I was surprised at how living abroad did this for me. You can, in time, find ways to put things into your resume that your peers will find too intriguing not to ask about. This is great for you, as you can prepare your story ahead and change the interview dynamic.

You can have the same effect with the skills you list, though this is a bit more challenging. Expect questions about every skill you list that is in line with the job posting. You may find that certain other skills also generate questions that you can similarly use to your advantage. Two examples that come to mind are mobile development and test-driven development. These two items have generated numerous conversations for me in interviews over the years. I've been more than happy to oblige with a well-practiced response.

Skills-Based Resume and Friends

I recommend building what I call a skills-based resume. There are others I'll cover at the end of this section, but I want to spend time covering the type of resume I think works very well in software development.

If you transition away from software development, you'll likely need one of the others. I'll include them for completeness' sake, but for now, let's pretend that skills-based is the only one.

A skills-based resume emphasizes the technical knowledge or skills you have in combination with practical experience. You might be thinking that this is your first job and that you don't have those things. Bear with me. You have a lot more than you think.

The basic layout I recommend in a skills-based resume is this:

1. Skills and Knowledge
2. Awards, Speaking, Relevant certifications
3. Experience
4. Education & Miscellaneous

Skills and Knowledge

Skills and knowledge come first for a reason. These are the things the HR professional and hiring manager are going to look for first. Don't make them search. Give them the goods right out of the gate. Are you applying for a job that requires React? Put it in your skills section if you can without lying. Do they want to see experience with agile development? Put that up there too.

I break my skills section down into three sub-sections. First are the technical skills. These are things like programming languages or source-control. Then come the frameworks and libraries. Here I put things like React, Spring, JBoss, etc. Last I have things like techniques or knowledge. Here I put things like agile development, automated testing, design patterns, etc. Those three sections have worked well for me, so find your way of splitting those things up.

If you're not sure what makes sense, you'll likely see common patterns after reading job descriptions for a while. They'll almost always include some fundamental technology backed with specific frameworks or libraries, and then ask for specific knowledge or techniques. See what makes sense.

As a small aside, every word you choose matters. If you're applying for a Java job and you can put it down without lying, put it first. Don't make them read to the end of a large list of things that don't matter.

Last, this skills section isn't every single skill. They're the ones you are choosing to emphasize. I phrase mine *Selected Skills*. I want to imply that I'm only showing the things that are relevant while having more to offer. Also, if you try to list everything you'll annoy the reader, and remember you only have sixty seconds of their attention.

Outstanding Awards and Other Flash

For the first time job-seekers, this section may be omitted depending on your background. I put this second because if you have something you can use to highlight excellence then put it here. Maybe you got an award at a different job. Maybe you've done some public speaking. Maybe you're published. You decide what and how you want to show those things off, but if you can keep it short and sweet put it here.

I list an award I received in college, though I have since pushed it further down in my resume to make room for other things. Now I have certifications and public speaking that I put in its place.

The point is that you can use this spot to show off a little. I recommend doing it now because you've already shown you have the skills, now show them your excellence. After that, they can learn more about the impact you've made.

Experience

This is where you'll spend the most time and energy on your resume. Learning how to present your experience, even if it isn't software-related, is going to take time, practice, and a lot of refinement.

Before I go further, remember what I said about length? It doesn't matter. I do want you to try filling out at least one full page. Beyond that, go crazy.

The name of the game with writing about your experience is to write with an outcome or impact in mind. This is a sharp contrast to listing the activities, tasks, or duties you did on the job. It separates you from everyone else by showing that while everyone else writes code, you create more profit, customers, and so-on. It takes practice and time to learn how to write this way, but it will distinguish you quickly.

Let's have an example contrasting the outcome-based experience statements from task-based ones.

Task-based
> Developed software across the entire tech stack

Outcome-based
> Developed software product that led to a 20% increase in customers

Put yourself in the shoes of someone who can only hire a few people to add to their team. If you had to pick between a resume that listed task-based experience or an outcome-based resume, you'd be drawn to the one who wrote outcome-based experience.

It is natural to feel like you cannot come up with any kind of outcome for what you've been doing. This takes time, practice, and reflection to identify. So we start the practice here. Here is a way to get started. Imagine telling a stranger about the project or the job you had. Try to complete the phrase, "We accomplished," or "We set out to accomplish." This will get you closer to the outcome you attempted to deliver. You may feel like you can't claim that outcome, but you did play an active role in achieving it. You may also realize that this outcome wasn't achieved while you were there. That is ok as well because you can word your experience in a way to reflect that. You may, through your reflection, also note that there were other impacts or outcomes. That is wonderful as they give you more material.

Here is a list of potential outcomes you might find in your experience and history so far:

- Financial gain or protection from loss
- Cost-cutting or efficiency gains
- Improvements to process
- Handoff reductions
- On-time, on-budget delivery
- Customer delight
- Customer acquisition or retention
- Increased community engagement
- Removal of defects

The list is endless for what you can find, but this list is here to get you thinking about what outcomes you can find and speak to in your experience.

You'll spend most of your resume-building effort trying to pinpoint the outcomes and tie them back to the job you had. Take the time to find your outcomes.

Now, in terms of how to write your experience sections, there are a few key elements to put down.

- Company
- Dates worked (Year is fine)
- Title
- Bulleted, outcome-oriented list

For the company, dates worked, and title you can list them all together in any way that is easy to read, and below that the experience follows.

When it comes to how many bulleted outcome-oriented items to put down, I advocate for two things. First, that you keep the number fairly consistent across your jobs, this may have no impact on anything whatsoever, but it gives an appearance of tidiness to your resume, and I think setting a few limits helps refine the impact on the few that you have. Second, I recommend that you stay somewhere between 3-5 bulleted items per job.

Putting all that together you may have something, though not formatted well, that looks something like this:

Acme Widgets

2018-Present

Software Wizard

- Co-created architecture of software product that gained 30k users in its first quarter
- Developed data transformation pipeline that processed 250 million records every day
- Implemented automated testing suites that removed serious production defects prior to release

And just for comparison, a similar task-oriented one that your competition will use:

Acme Widgets

2018-Present

Software Wizard

- Architected software platform using Spring, Java, React
- Developed ETL process using Hadoop
- Wrote automated unit tests

Hopefully, this contrast seems extreme, if not comically so. While I made up these examples to point out the differences, the task-oriented example is very common to see in the wild. As you begin to see others' resumes, you'll see the same thing, unless they read this book. Even a few outcome-based bullets will put you in the pile of people a manager wants to talk to over the person whose experience amounts to "Showed up to work."

You may have noticed that in the outcome-based example, I didn't mention any specific technologies that were in play to achieve those outcomes. The reason is that, in the broader picture of this resume format, you can list the skills and technologies you want to be interviewed on there. Listing them here in the experience is redundant. Also, by leaving them off, you have a bit more freedom with the story you tell when someone asks you about that experience.

You can use your skills section to highlight the ones relevant to the job posting mixed with others you can speak to and impress them with. You use your experience to show that you're more than someone who writes code and you have a chance to tell a story beyond the technologies you used. If you mentioned technology in those experience bullets, you might be asked very specific questions regarding the technology's role and limitations in achieving the outcome.

We'll cover this idea about controlling the interviews in the interviewing chapters. For now though, writing your experience in a way that invites a question like, "Tell me how you did that," is preferable to, "What scaling limitations did you bump into using Hadoop?" One is a story, and the other is a test.

Other Resume Formats

There are two other types of resumes[5] that exist, but they have their uses outside of getting a software job.

First, is a purely experiential resume, sometimes called a chronological or traditional resume. This resume relies almost entirely on your experience starting from now and working backward. After a few years, you may find this resume format makes sense. In the beginning, you won't have enough relevant experience to rely solely on that. To get through the HR professional, you'll have to mix your keywords into those sections carefully to not be too overt about it, but also allow them to find the information they need to move on.

The other major type of resume you'll see is a functional resume. This resume is all about saying what you can do. Again, you'll note the format I've provided contains this element in a skills section. A functional resume takes this a bit further though and will sometimes have a summary section where you try to very convincingly list the traits, qualities, and skills you bring to a situation. There may be no experience on resumes like this. This resume may sound perfect for the first-time job-hunter, but in truth, it is very challenging to write in a way that looks reasonable.

If you transition to management, you'll likely find this style of resume is more common and want to build one yourself. In this format, you can outline a summary of your accomplishments as a leader, then highlight the skills and traits you have, and finally, list

---

[5]https://blog.simplyhired.com/jobsearch/resumes/3-main-types-resumes/

experience if you choose. Again, as you see more and more resumes on the job and in the wild, you'll get a feel for the styles that exist.

Technically the one I offered is a combination but has served well over the years for myself and others. Feel free to experiment over time with yours. The name of the game is to build a resume that gets you an interview.

But I Don't Have Experience

This statement gets its own section. You do have experience, but you aren't aware of it yet. I want to be very clear about what experience is and is not.

Experience is not just writing code.

Experience is what you bring from your education and work history that is valuable to a company.

Every job you've had so far, or projects that you've been on at school, or internships, or open-source projects you've worked on are fair game. You'll want to emphasize the experience that resulted in a paycheck, but it is all fair game.

So then what do you do with all of this non-development experience? Well, this is where things get interesting. Here are several non-development skills and traits that are extremely important and seldom emphasized.

- Organizing groups of people
- Clear and concise communication
- Teamwork
- Problem-solving
- Helping get decisions made
- Supporting organizational goals
- Growth and learning

- Working with clients and customers
- Discovering new products
- Trying new things
- Teaching
- Mentoring
- Being great to work with
- Becoming competent quickly
- Working through stressful situations
- Handling a crisis
- Making a difficult decision
- Finding new tools or techniques
- Providing measurements
- Meeting commitments
- Accepting responsibility

Many managers and companies are hungry for these traits, and you can easily highlight them from any previous job now that you know they are desirable. So yes, that summer job where you flipped burgers can be part of your resume when you show that you were able to handle the stress of the job and mentor new employees.

In my resume, I highlighted a few specific experiences I thought would be intriguing, or invite questions, and I was right. One was teaching English abroad, and another was ocean lifeguarding. The first would prompt questions about what it was like to live in Japan. I'd give a five-minute talk about what it was like there and weave in stories about how I developed new training material and rose to become the supervisor in the company. For the second they'd want to know if the job was like Baywatch, and I'd tell some stories to emphasize my willingness to train and how I could handle literal life-and-death situations.

The point is you can take your previous non-development experience and use it to show that you bring a lot more to the table than just technical ability. In fact, in several types of companies like agencies and consultancies, being able to work with customers and clients is incredibly valuable.

Adjustments and Experiments

Ok, at this point you have the basics of writing a resume. Start with your skills and knowledge. Follow that with any major accomplishments or awards. Move on to your experience and wrap up with education and other miscellaneous items.

The task at hand, if we remember back to the basic plan, is that now you have to write your first draft. Build a resume with these elements and pay attention to writing your experience so that it is outcome-oriented. This may take several passes.

When you read your resume, read each line in your experience and see if you can find ways to make it more impactful or powerful. Use numbers where you can as it hooks the mind of the reader.

When this is done, you have a prototype resume.

Going forward in the process you'll take this resume and then for each and every job you apply to you'll evaluate your resume again. Re-read it and see if there are some adjustments you can make to turn that dial up even higher. Sometimes, seeing it again after a little time gives new ideas.

Then make a few adjustments you think will help you stand out for the specific job at hand. Some simple ideas are to adjust the words in your skills section. Move the ones they emphasize to the front. If, as you research the company, you see how you could tweak your experience to line up with something that you've learned, make that adjustment as well.

Don't spend too long doing this, but you'll likely find that you'll make a lot of small adjustments early on which will slowly taper off as you get more and more interviews. That's because you've honed your resume to the point that it is almost a given your phone will ring after you send it in.

This process will start over if you apply to different industries, positions, or tech-stack. This takes less time than you'd think, so don't hesitate to try. You'll notice, for instance, that financial institutions are interested in different skills than a start-up would be. Your resume will change based on that. If you go from back-end to front-end development things will change again. As you improve your resume writing it'll be only a little extra work to start getting interviews with a new resume.

In terms of organization, I keep my prototype resume separate from the ones I use when I apply. That's because I write my prototype resume with more bullets and more skills than I apply with. This serves as a menu I can use to tailor my resume specifically to the job I'm applying for.

Tricks and Gotchas

I realized as I was concluding this chapter that there are a few items I want to mention specifically. These are miscellaneous practices I've learned that won't change much in the long run, but they're part of my process, so I'll put them in here.

First, only submit your resume as PDF. You'll sometimes get asked to send it in a Word format. Recruiters are notorious for asking this. PDF will always display the same no matter where someone looks at it. That means all the formatting you've done will be exactly the way it was when you wrote it. If you submit using something like Word, then it may change drastically based on the software versions they have. Don't take that chance.

You may also remember the story I told of someone who looks at all the invisible characters in a resume to see how consistently and correctly the applicant formatted their resume. They can do it in Word. They can't do that in a PDF. While I doubt I'll encounter anyone else that does this, I was comforted knowing that my PDF habit would have prevented an early disqualification.

Next—and this is a key reason to submit your resume in a non-editable format—recruiters are notorious for changing your resume. At their most benign, they'll simply put it into their format and stationery. More commonly they'll reformat and then truncate it to fit within two pages. Less commonly they'll alter the contents to make sure you have all the keywords sprinkled throughout the resume. I cannot stand this behavior. Also, they'll rarely tell you they do this. You'll find out after you see your resume on the job. Believe me, it can be a shock to see your name on a resume you don't recognize.

I was at one company and saw my resume in a file of resumes as I began to interview people. I noticed it had my name on it, but it had been reformatted entirely. I asked to look at it, and my jaw dropped. Years of experience were missing, pieces of the experiences that I did have were missing. This was not my resume. This was some hack job with my name on top. I gave my manager a copy of my resume and asked if they had any idea these recruiters were doing that. The thought had never crossed their mind.

Let's talk about references. The rule here is that references are available upon request. They are used less often than you'd think and they are a pain in the butt. Also, you know when they are likely going to pick up the phone and call someone. You can give your references a heads-up that they may get a call soon. This is a courtesy. Nobody likes getting a call out of the blue from some random number only to be put on the spot to give their opinion of you to a total stranger.

Last up is some formatting tips. I mentioned above that I aim for readability. I like a very even and clean looking resume. Your three primary tools for doing that are an established template, tables, or tab-stops.

Starting with a template is the easiest way to begin if you find one you like that isn't obnoxious. See if there is one that speaks to you and looks clean. Then fill it out and make it your own.

Tables are a way for you to create columns on a page. So, for example, you may want to list your experience where your company is on the left and the years worked on the right. Inserting a table into the page and adjusting the columns can give you that effect nicely. The downside is that working with tables can be a major pain.

Last up are tab-stops. These are like a poor version of tables. Essentially you can use tab-stops to control how much indentation happens on a line. This combined with right, left, and center justification can give you a similar effect to tables. The main thing here is that you can get some odd effects when you adjust a tab stop and use a bulleted list.

Maybe start with a template.

So for now, write that prototype resume or, if you're re-reading this chapter, dust yours off and clean it up!

4 - Cover Letters

Ah, cover letters! The lingering vestiges of an old hiring process. This chapter, admittedly, was a bit of a struggle to place. It had a second home with portfolios and the other secondary material, but I decided to keep it out on its own due to how prominent it is in my current process today.

This chapter will aim to include everything you need to know about writing cover letters. The good news is that over time it takes a lot less effort than you may think. The bad news is that it will take a bit of effort the first few times while you get the hang of it.

I've written a cover letter for every single job I've applied to. Now, in most job-seeking endeavors there is very little feedback available to help one navigate the process. So how do I know they're worth the time? I have had interviews based solely on my cover letters. I've received feedback directly during interviews, and that has reinforced this practice for me all these years.

They Matter

Aside from my anecdote, why are cover letters still useful today? Well, think of all the artifacts we put in front of future employers as currency to purchase their time and consideration. A resume purchases around sixty seconds.

A cover letter can purchase a few minutes. Portfolios can buy a few more, as can a GitHub profile, social media accounts, and so on. So if we think of it from that perspective, cover letters are a good investment of our time because they yield minutes of return back from the employer.

Starting, it won't feel this way. Writing cover letters will take time, far more than the minutes it buys you. Like all skills though, this will get easier and easier with practice. Like the prototype resume, you'll have cover letters you can adjust for each job.

Let's look at this another way as well. Let's pretend that after reading your resume a hiring manager has two total resumes to consider for interviews, yours and another. The hiring manager views your resumes as equals, even though they couldn't be more different. How will he decide who to call in? Well, if you provided a cover letter, you will have the opportunity to tell a story that enhances what he read in the resume, explain perceived weaknesses, and amplify your strengths. For the person who didn't write one, their sixty seconds of consideration is over.

Cover letters provide you a blank piece of paper that you can use to tell your story on your terms in your voice. You can become a real person with experiences, hopes, dreams, and strengths far beyond what a resume could show. You can write your story in a way that removes all doubt that you're the candidate they want to hire.

A cover letter is an unscripted and unformatted way for you to show your potential employer who you can become.

This potential is thrown away by so many applicants as they believe cover letters are outdated. While I cannot argue that they are old-fashioned, the potential impact they have is enormous. For the time it takes, isn't it worth a shot to write one?

Who Reads Them

This question is a little tricky to answer as it varies wildly. You can minimally assume the hiring manager will, though I've met some who throw them away and refuse to read them. We can't please everyone in this process, but we can make it as favorable as we can.

I've never met someone who threw a candidate out for submitting one.

Beyond the hiring manager, it is hard to predict who will read them. So the safest course of action is to plan for them, but think that someone else may see it too. The one exception to this that I'd put forward is that the HR professional may read it, but aside from filtering for profanity and other objectionable material, it is unlikely they will have a loud voice about the cover letter.

That leaves us with the question of how much time will we buy from a hiring manager and, therefore, how long should we write it? Well, in my experience it needs to stay on one page. I tend to keep my cover letters to around three paragraphs which in total, runs around three-quarters of a page.

These three paragraphs don't present a massive opportunity for an expansive and enthralling story, but it is enough to hit the major highlights effectively. That is the goal; just like with writing a resume, we are distilling things down to their most potent elements.

If you feel compelled to write more than a page, you have creative license to do what you'd like with cover letters, but I cannot be your guide in that territory. You may knock it out of the park. I'll share a story in a little bit of one such case.

A Great Cover Letter

To me, there are two basic types of cover letters: Simple and creative. The elements that allow either to work are your sincerity, skill, and knowledge of your employer.

Sincerity is about writing in a way that shows people who you are. It lets the reader approach you as a person before they ever meet you. Your writing can convey the traits of who you are, your humor, your professionalism, and anything else you want, in a way few other things can. Writing with sincerity is a beautiful opportunity to show an employer that you're the right fit for their company beyond the expertise they want. The key is to write in a way that is true to who you are.

Skill, in this case, is going to boil down to your use of language. So, run your letter through spellcheck and any grammar checker. Look for words you repeat a lot and alter them. Read it and see if it has a good flow or if there is a sentence that seems to mess everything up. That may be a bit specific to how I write, but you get the idea. Your cover letter doesn't have to be perfect, but it can't be wrong. As with resumes, submit this in a PDF as well.

Knowledge of your employer pertains to the homework you've done about them ahead of applying. Minimally you want to read their website's main pages. Read the about section, learn about their careers and why they think it is so great to be there. If the job posting has a portion about the company, pay attention there. If they have a news section, skim that too for any significant news in the past six months. Get a feel for who they are and the traits they value the most. They will very likely spell that out for you. When writing your cover letter, take the opportunity to highlight those same traits that you have as well. Connect the dots between those traits, your skills, and experience on your resume.

Simple Cover Letter

As for the two types of letters, let's begin with a simple one. This format is essentially a few paragraphs that cover what is in your resume as a story. You get to put more color and life to the powerful experience statements in your resume by telling a more profound and richer story about how that specific experience makes you even more of a fit for your employer and how you're on an even better trajectory.

The basic structure of this cover letter has three basic paragraphs:

1. Establishing Fit

2. Your Experience
3. Summation

The first paragraph quickly establishes why you are a fit for the position. You can do this by highlighting a quick fact from your experience to grab attention. You can do it with a well-crafted mission statement or a compelling dream of yours. The first paragraph is there to get the hiring manager to read the rest, and cement in their mind that you're the person for the job.

The second paragraph goes deep into your experience. This paragraph can get away from you when writing it, as it is tempting to include more and more experience. Resist the temptation. For each piece of experience you want to highlight, keep it to one or two sentences at most. I choose which experiences to use based on how I want to emphasize the skills and qualities they're looking for. If they value people who take the initiative, I highlight that aspect in one or two sentences. Since this is a single paragraph, you'll have to limit this to two or three items, or you'll create a wall of text nobody will want to read.

The last paragraph sums everything up. You want to put everything to a focal point showing how you have the skills, ambition, and qualities that are the perfect match for the employer now and for years to come.

Now, the first time you write this, it may take an hour or more. As you do this more often it will take less. You'll also find that you are writing similar things over and over. This pattern indicates you may be able to create a more extensive cover letter that you can use as a menu to more quickly build job-specific ones and edit your way to a great cover letter. Getting to this point will take numerous attempts.

Creative Cover Letter

The creative cover letter is an entirely different animal. This cover letter is what happens when you feel like taking a significant risk. The significant risk is that your application gets thrown in the garbage can immediately.

I find myself willing to take that risk at least one time in a job search. Maybe it's me wanting to blow off steam in the process. Either way, at some point I'll write the cover letter that makes me happy instead of the one I know I should.

The rule here is: If it makes you smile, write it.

That's it. Go crazy. Write what your heart is telling you. Write what the insane voice in your head is yelling. Write the cover letter that nobody would ever hire you for, but it'd be a great story if they did. Within that advice to enjoy the freedom, don't be insulting or rude.

Here is a line that I started one such cover letter with. "Know what is more awesome than T-Rexes skating on F-16s while double-fisting A-1 sauce? Me."

I won't even try to defend writing that. There was no master plan or strategy. It made me smile. Plenty of people shook their heads at me. The point of me sharing that is to point out that this type of cover letter is for you to let go of convention and take a risk. This cover letter is art and expression. Your audience may not want it.

Do They Work?

Remember when I wrote that absurd thing about T-Rexes? That cover letter got me an interview.

Plenty others I've written I've also heard nothing about, one way or another. That absurd cover letter is an exception. That one cemented in my mind that cover letters are worth writing if it improves the chance of getting an interview at all.

Don't take this anecdote to mean that if you write a creative cover letter that you will have a better chance, I've written plenty of absurd letters that never got me an interview. Do take this to mean that a cover letter—traditional or creative—can improve your chances.

5 - Portfolios, GitHub, and Other Friends

The industry seems to be changing in terms of what it asks potential candidates to provide. All over the internet, you'll find people talking about portfolios, their GitHub activity, and other elements as key to getting a job. I take a somewhat controversial stance by saying that these materials are secondary concerns to a great resume and interviewing skills.

Within this chapter, I break down various secondary items you can add to your overall presentation when you apply for a job.

Their Place in The Plan

If you recall back to *The Plan* where I outlined the plan from a high level, working on these items comes well after you start applying for jobs. That list is ordered explicitly to provide focus and priority to a job-seeker. I want your first focus to be on resumes. The idea is to create a routine practice of searching and applying for jobs. As the number of interviews you receive begins to climb, you'll be developing your secondary materials.

I emphasize having a great resume as the core of my plan because it will communicate your skills and convince them to look at your secondary materials. You absolutely can get an interview without a portfolio or GitHub activity or a great LinkedIn. And you might interview more with some mix of these thrown in. Once you have that prototype resume and you're applying to jobs, let's enhance your chances of getting an interview.

Shifting the Odds

Throughout this book, I've framed the job-search process as collecting yeses and avoiding noes. These secondary materials help increase the chances of getting a yes at the crucial stage when someone chooses to interview you or not. They don't get you a job or an offer—but these materials aid in getting you an interview.

Pretend your resume, cover letter, and application are sitting next to one other person's. If the resumes and cover letters were the same—which they aren't if you've followed my advice—they might still need to find a way to decide between you. Your resume lists a portfolio site. Theirs doesn't. You win, provided that your portfolio doesn't create a reason for them to walk away. Yours may give a link to an active GitHub account where they can see that you've been actively contributing to projects that are in use. Yours may link to a LinkedIn profile that allows them to know how you're connected professionally, or if you have any endorsements. You may have listings of times you've spoken at meetups and conferences, and they'll think that you must know your stuff. They'll choose you in these cases.

The entire point of these secondary materials is to increase your odds. They help give assurance and further highlight what you're capable of when there is no previous relevant work history.

There is a golden rule to all of this which I must highlight.

Everything you show must highlight how good you are for them.

If you go in with a "Build it, and they will come," mentality, you'll find yourself frustrated and jobless. Each element you create provides a specially curated experience designed to lead them to the same outcome every time: You're the right person for the job. However, if you show a portfolio and it is ugly, you are better off not showing it. Who decides if it's ugly? The hiring manager decides how ugly it is. If you have focused on GitHub, the developers and hiring manager determine whether the code you've contributed is quality or not.

Keep this in mind as we get into the details of building these elements out. We are building a crafted story that they take part in, and you're the heroine or hero they need.

Requested vs. Expected

The software industry is changing, and it can be hard to recognize what is unusual or standard when it comes to getting a job. You are likely to find a very inconsistent set of requests around social media accounts, portfolios, GitHub profiles, and more.

In this chaos, it can be hard to know the difference between what employers are asking for compared to what they expect.

For example, some companies ask for your social media handles and accounts. Some require it. I never give those out regardless. A few years ago, this was all over the news; employers were asking for Facebook accounts from future candidates. It can, in this process, begin to feel as though because they are requesting them that providing these things are typical and expected.

You always get to choose what you provide and how you present yourself. This means that you won't apply to certain companies. That's fine, and I encourage anyone to walk away from any job that seems off-putting or unpleasant.

Just because you see a blank for a link to your portfolio doesn't mean they expect you to have one. Employers accommodate for those that do. You are not necessarily less of a candidate for leaving that blank.

I don't have a portfolio. I don't share my GitHub or any social media with any employer. There were a handful of companies in the past that required these for application, so I terminated my applications and got a job somewhere else. Just because a company asks for secondary materials or social media handles doesn't mean you are obligated to provide anything.

Time Investment

Time to get real honest about what the cost of these materials is. It can take weeks or months to put up a portfolio site that creates the experience you want the viewer to have. It can take months to develop the right kind of GitHub activity to show meaningful and quality contributions to projects. It can take weeks or months to build a network and accumulate endorsements on LinkedIn.

It takes a considerable investment of time up front. The payoff is that you are more likely to get an interview. While I'm all for anything to improve your chances of getting an interview, I can't say that spending weeks and months on these materials is worth the payoff compared to the process I've outlined.

If I, for example, advocated that you build an exceptional portfolio as a critical element in your job-search process, I'd be asking you to spend weeks and months on creating a site before you'd even think about applying for an interview. The time investment it takes to build these secondary materials is far too unbalanced to do it first.

The Incomplete Menu

So far, I have mentioned portfolios, GitHub, and LinkedIn, but let's go a little further and list the items that you could use to show people how excellent you are beyond your resume.

- Portfolio

- GitHub
- LinkedIn
- Conference or Meetup talks
- Industry volunteering
- Competitions
- Training or certifications
- Publications
- Tutoring or teaching

If this list strikes you as surprisingly non-development-focused, you'd be correct. The only item in this list that shows your ability to write code is GitHub. Almost everything else indicates an investment in your industry. You might think the portfolio is an excellent demonstration of your development abilities, but you absolutely can build a remarkable portfolio with very little code.

Before going into specifics in the following sections, here is a brief description of each.

Portfolios are commonly a personal site that highlights your professional capabilities. They speak to the core of what you bring to a company, they show off that you know how to build a great site, and provide visuals that show off what else you can do as well.

GitHub activity is about consistency and content. The name of the game here is to show that you are active in your field. They can be your projects, or they can be a part of someone else's public project. Either way, you're showing off that you're developing code regularly, even when you aren't working.

Conferences and meetups talks are precisely that. Meetup talks are about getting in front of a room of people and sharing what you know. You'd be surprised how many meetups in your area are looking for speakers. If you tell your inner critic to be quiet for a minute, you'll find you have something to share. So share it and then make your employers aware that you have given talks. It will impress them.

Industry volunteering is all about connecting with local or national groups who need volunteers. There are likely a few STEM groups looking for volunteers. Their entire purpose is to get more people into the industry, especially women and other underrepresented populations. Go, volunteer! Continue volunteering after you get the job.

There are online competitions where you can join a team or compete as a solo developer to solve hard problems or complete projects in a short period. Some of them even have cash prizes. One such example with a cool factor to it is a Ludum Dare[6] or any game jam. Show off that you competed and what you did.

There is a whole world of training material, workshops, and certifications. I hope anyone going into this industry falls in love with learning anyway, but you may be able to use the training and workshops you've attended as evidence that you are committed to learning in the industry. Certifications are a bit of a trickier topic as there aren't many certifications that matter in software development, but this may change. One relatively new example is the Amazon Web Services certifications[7]. Getting this certificate would not be related to software development, but will show that you could handle cloud operations professionally.

Publication may seem like a dying art, but I believe the target has moved from print to respected online outlets. The goal here is to publish your writing online so that people can see what you know, how you communicate, and what kind of following you have. Many websites can accommodate this exact purpose. Start publishing material if you're interested in writing. Eventually, something will take off, and then you can hold the accomplishment up proudly. How wild would it be to get an interview where someone quotes information from an article you wrote?

Last, but not least is teaching and tutoring. These two are similar

---

[6]https://ludemdare.com
[7]https://aws.amazon.com/certification/

to volunteering, except you might receive compensation. The idea here is helping someone else learn the ropes of the industry. If you can point to an established or professional-looking teaching and tutoring relationship, you can easily use it to show that you've learned the material well enough to teach it. Teaching is a highly prized skill in senior developers.

The Rules

For each of these elements, we aim to tell a particular story to our audience. The story is that you are exceptional and the only real choice among all the candidates available.

There are a few guidelines I'll to direct you toward as you consider building anything. These, when taken seriously, will help keep the time investment to a minimum while maximizing their effectiveness.

- Less is more
- Only show what you can sell
- It isn't about you

"Less is more" is calling to the idea that if you had to choose between ten half-complete items or two complete items, we prefer the two. Aiming for a vast and complex portfolio or an extensive chronology in GitHub is overly ambitious for getting an interview. We want to distill down our efforts to only a few well-done items instead of a large project.

When it comes to only showing what you can sell, I recommend you make sure that whatever you leave out for people to find isn't something that will work against you. If you have a typo in the about page of your portfolio, that's a problem. If your GitHub activity is full of a bunch of half-baked projects that don't run, that's a problem. Get the idea? Put your best foot forward with the items you choose to present.

The last principle serves as a reminder that your portfolio is for your audience. This isn't about you. These items aren't here for you to show off everything you've done or how good you think you are. They exist to get your audience excited. Excite them with the material you present. Make them want to pick up the phone and call you.

Getting Started

Portfolios

Even if you are unsure if building a portfolio is right for you, the broad answer will be that it *is* right for you.

If your focus is in an area of software where presentation is a concern, like mobile or the web, then your portfolio must be visually well-presented. If you are more focused on back-end or server development, you may be able to develop a portfolio that is simple and unobtrusive.

Let's look at some essential ways to start with a portfolio. First, don't solve any problems that are invisible to the casual observer. I've met some developers who decide to set up an entire server by hand to host their portfolio. Nobody can see this, so don't bother. This advice extends to building your portfolio with some invisible frameworks or libraries. If you can't easily show that you made your site using React, for example, and React is unfamiliar to your audience, then don't bother. Building a good experience trumps any technical feat you attempt to show off.

Since your portfolio site is essentially the marketing of yourself, there are a few key design elements I want to bring to your attention. First, your landing page is the first and most lasting impression you make. Make it easy to find examples of your work, your passion, who you are, and how to contact you. Don't make them scroll for critical information. These are the necessary elements in a portfolio.

If you need design help, there are plenty of free designs you can use to get started. Be aware of copyright and attribution rules as you do this. I have no sense of design myself, so I will often look through many designs before I find something I can take apart and put back together my way.

Since you are building this to excite someone, I want you to spend more time on distilling who you are into a brief message that is no more than a sentence or two. Crafting a clear statement takes time to do well. You can expound more about yourself on your about page, but when describing yourself and passions, aim for short, clear, and compelling sentences.

You may think you don't have any work to show off yet. That may be true, and your only example will be the portfolio site itself. If that is the case, don't link to examples that are "Under Construction" or empty. Just don't have it.

Distilling all of this down, your portfolio is only an opportunity to show off technologies if you make them visible. Follow the basic design guidelines I described where you have the most significant impact—on the first landing page. Don't make people scroll. Have examples of work, your passions, information about you, and how to contact you.

One of the principles is to show only things that sell you. I want to highlight a common problem I find in a lot of portfolios. JavaScript warnings and errors are like having a spelling error in your resume. Since you're applying to a development job, assume that your future peers know how to open a development console and look at your code to the extent that it is visible. They'll look at the HTML and the CSS. Keep it clean and well done. Don't let laziness here be the reason you don't get the interview.

If you'd like a little more information, Ali Spittel[8] offers some good basics and provides examples to other portfolios that are worth a look.

GitHub

Using GitHub for secondary material gives people a sneak peek into the kind of code you produce and the projects you have joined.

You can have a tremendous amount of activity without contributing anything except to your own projects. This activity is great. I recommend that the only projects you make publicly visible are the ones you want to share with potential employers.

If that last statement makes you a little nervous, that is understandable. There is advice in *The Interview Stages* about take-home assignments you may want to read regarding how to get your code up to snuff quickly. The basics are: ensure it's formatted consistently, comment anything that isn't obvious at a glance, and keep functions and classes small. Having automated tests earn bonus points almost anywhere. Also, a readme that is idiot-proof for getting the project running is exceptional.

If that sounds like a lot of overhead, that's because while it is somewhat representative of the career to do those things, you are in a position to be judged right now. Don't leave yourself open to an adverse judgment for something you can fix with a little extra time.

You may find that of the projects you've started, only a few are worth cleaning up. That is fine. In fact, you may want to start just a few small ones from scratch that are purpose-built to show what you can do and make the rest private. You're creating a curated experience to show developers and hiring managers that you finish what you start and code well.

---

[8]Spittel, Ali. "Building a Kickass Portfolio" Dev.to. https://dev.to/aspittel/building-a-kick-ass-portfolio-28ph (accessed December 26, 2019)

Keep your projects very small. You might even want to think of them as demos or proofs-of-concept. What you'll have is maybe a handful of small projects that show off some concept or demonstrate how something might work. None of this is a full-blown application or running in production, but it does allow you to have a complete piece of software.

There is another way to leverage GitHub beyond your projects—contribute to other projects. I don't have a lot of specific advice to give here as I'm not an expert. Was I an interviewer, I'd look to see what kinds of projects you've contributed to in terms of popularity and interest, and then what types of contributions you've made.

Ultimately, contribute to anything you like, but if you want to start contributing to a more recognizable project, I recommend that you begin by updating their documentation. It isn't glamorous, but people overlook it, and it is often easy to get approval. Updating documentation earns you credibility with moderators and maintainers that may expedite your way into submitting code changes.

To recap, if you choose to use GitHub as a part of your application package, keep things small, well done, and highlight your ability to complete software projects professionally.

LinkedIn & Social Media

LinkedIn is the Facebook of professionals. You can build connections to people you've never met through professional relationships, host your resume, engage in groups, chat, and look for jobs.

Using LinkedIn as a part of your application package is pretty limited. You can present it if you have a reasonably connected network and if you come with endorsements.

When someone looks at your profile, LinkedIn will tell them how closely connected they are to you and how those connections exist.

If your network connects you through someone the interviewer respects, that looks good for you. It also feels better for the interviewer to know that the person they're interviewing is a known entity.

One potential benefit of LinkedIn is that compared to a lot of the other items in this list, LinkedIn is a pretty short path to creating a network and getting some endorsements. So, if everything else seems daunting, consider starting with LinkedIn.

I mentioned before that some companies will ask for your social media accounts as a part of the application and that I don't give those out. Even if you don't give them away, you are likely very easy to find online. You may want to take a quick inventory of what you've put out online recently.

On the one hand, your online presence is yours. So, if that is your frame of mind, then there is nothing to cause worry. Alternatively, you may see some newer things that you don't want everyone to find quickly. Consider making your profiles private while you're on the job hunt or remove particularly questionable posts. This level of paranoia is optional, and advice I don't follow. When companies search for me online, they know what they are getting.

Conference or Meetup Talks & Publications

I started speaking at conferences nationally in 2018. That decision opened more doors than I can count. It is quite common that someone offers me a job at every conference where I speak—nothing in writing though.

Speaking at an event allows you to share your experience, knowledge, and skill with a broad audience. When you are the speaker, you are in a position people respect. This position can be a massive boon to a job-seeker.

Getting started at conferences can be a bit of a long process but speaking at a local Meetup[9] could be very quick. Many gatherings are so starved for speakers that you could very easily find yourself in front of a room of people one evening sharing your story.

While this book isn't about getting started in public speaking, I do want to say this: Your experience is worth sharing. Your knowledge is something people want.

Standing in front of a room full of people from your community and speaking means that people are watching you. Some of them may know their companies are hiring. If your message lands with them, they'll want you to work with them too. People will line up to speak with you. Having a line of people waiting to meet you is a potent way to network very quickly.

Consider speaking locally. It's a great way to meet people and show off what you can do. You can also use the experience of speaking on your resume in the place where you might put awards. It shows you have some industry presence. Companies are generally pretty excited to find out that their employees speak at conferences and local groups. It's great marketing and brand exposure for them.

Industry volunteering & Teaching

Many software development organizations need volunteers. Find them and get to work. Not only are you giving back, but they are giving you stories and experience that shows you can contribute in more ways than just code.

Teaching falls into the same essential category. As you move up the ladder to a senior software developer, your expectations will change. Mentoring and guiding more junior developers will be a part of your job. Showing that you already can and do teach other

---

[9]https://meetup.com

developers quickly identifies that you have traits they would want in a more senior person.

Also, if you can teach something, whether through volunteering or a paid teaching program, it shows that you have a certain level of mastery over the concept, so if you teach back-end server development using Java and Spring Boot, that tells people that you command enough expertise to show others that same thing. Depending on your area of focus, this will be a straightforward story to show an employer that you know what you're doing.

Also, the experience of working with people in a volunteer or teaching environment will force you to practice thinking through technical problems on your feet. The questions you'll be asked will help you gain the confidence you need to navigate technical interviews as well.

Competition

Remember back in the resume section where I recommended that you list awards and other accolades right after your skills? Imagine having in that section a small bit saying that you've placed within a coding competition.

Participating in a competition where you place or can show that you completed it can be an easy way to confirm that your skills and knowledge exist at a competitive level and that your passions extend beyond the hum-drum of a job. It will take some work on your part to also tell a compelling story around the competition and your efforts, but it can be a great way to generate interest in you as a candidate while also having some fun.

When I was in college, I took part in a global competition held by IBM. I thought my submission was terrible, and I didn't want to win. The grand prize seemed more like work than a reward, whereas the other placements were interesting. I targeted the

2nd place prize and succeeded. I got the award I wanted, which happened to be an iPod. For years afterward, I featured that I placed in a global competition proudly on my resume and received enough questions during interviews that the payoff from the competition was worth a lot more than an iPod.

If this sounds interesting to you, search out any coding competition, enter, and compete. Admittedly these kinds of competitions make me feel stupid and insecure, but if I approach them with the attitude that it is a challenge for myself, and that the payoff may be a prize or a better job, then it is easier to enter.

Another benefit to these competitions is that they will, by their very nature, force you to solve tricky programming problems. Competitions also serve as great practice to get through stressful technical interviews while possibly reaping the benefits of winning a prize and using it on your resume. You may even find simpler versions of the questions you have to solve during interviews!

The downside with this particular avenue is that within the industry there aren't many competitions with name-brand recognition. So, even if you win some competition that is by all accounts remarkable, the person who sees your information may have no idea how remarkable it is. That's why this approach is secondary to a great resume.

When you can mention that you've won an award or competition, it hooks the reader into the possibility that you're a lot more than you seem and makes them want to find out about the competition. It sets you up to tell a riveting story about your endeavors in a coding competition and how you were able to succeed. That story can highlight so many great qualities and strengths.

Training or Certifications

Last but not least are training and certifications. When it comes to software development, the truth is that this category amounts to very little. There are currently no certifications that anyone cares about for software development, and training is a tough sell to a potential employer.

I mention it because training can be used to highlight how invested you are in your career and development within it. Many developers you encounter will invest nothing in their continued education when it comes to training. Showing an employer that you are committed enough to spend money on growing your skills can be a very compelling story.

Further, depending on what kind of software development you want to do, you may find that there are complimentary certifications or training that are worth taking. For example, if you were a front-end developer, part of your skillset will be making a great experience for people through the web. Showing that you are able to complement your technical skills with training in UX or Design Thinking could be an exciting way to show that you're expanding your abilities towards more of the interaction and solution space. If you are a back-end developer, pursuing training in more operational or DevOps material would show a similar expansion of skill beyond just building the server application to also being able to operationalize and scale it.

There are no guarantees here, but it is worth considering if you have the money and opportunity to do so.

Conclusion

There are a lot of secondary materials you can add to your resume-cover letter package. Each one of these has the potential to shift the odds to your favor when you produce something that looks good in the eyes of a hiring manager.

After you have a handle on your resume and cover letter, pick one of these and add it to your package to put in front of employers. It can be a significant time investment, but if it improves your chances, then it is worth a try.

The name of the game is to make the people considering you say yes. Put your best examples forward, think of the story you'll tell, and apply.

6 - Applying for Jobs

By now, we've covered building a great resume, writing cover letters, and a whole lot of secondary materials that you can add to your application package. Now it is time to dig into the process of applying for jobs.

This chapter outlines how to find jobs, how to read the postings, research the company and position, how to leverage your network, and stay organized through this process. Remember, in the plan I've laid out you'll apply to three jobs a week. This chapter shows you how to do it well.

Strategy

Before I get into the details I've just outlined, I want to explain in a bit more depth how the application process works concerning the plan that I described in *The Plan*.

In that chapter, I recommend that you apply to three jobs a week. I further went to say that the reason you do this is to get a lot of practice with interviewing and to get feedback on your application package. When it comes to practice, you can and will receive advice on how to practice technical interviewing at home. That will carry you only so far before the nerves of having to answer questions or whiteboard on the spot undo your practice. Improving interview skills happens best through actually interviewing.

Also, when interviewing, you'll get a much better feel for the kinds of questions that you will need to practice. While it is relatively easy to find a list of preparation questions online and in this book, in practice, you'll find a recurring set for the type of software development you're targeting. By interviewing, you'll begin to see common questions that you can practice.

Your application package is your best guess at what will score an interview. You'll only know they are working in your favor when you get called for an interview. So, by applying regularly, you're continually validating whether your application package is improving or not. You can hone that package so precisely that you'll get an interview nearly every time you apply.

Now, let's move beyond that into some other reasons I recommend applying for jobs so aggressively. The reality is that if you apply for three posts a week, you will have to submit for positions that do not excite you. Applying for uninteresting jobs is a crucial piece of this whole strategy. When you submit your application to a post you aren't interested in, you similarly won't be hurt if you're rejected or ghosted. You won't be as nervous about the interview for a job you don't particularly want.

I often say that the job you're best prepared to get is the one you don't want. I say this because of how much more calm, confident, and situationally aware you can be when you can walk away from the job. By applying over-and-over, you'll be in that position more often than not. That way, when you do apply for an exciting role, you will enter that interview far more collected than if the dream job were the only one you were considering.

There is also an element of this that I'll cover in *The Interview Stages*, but a crucial part of interviewing is you interviewing the employer. There are enough terrible jobs out there that learning to detect them quickly is a vital skill to apply during interviews. When you go into an interview for a job you're not interested in, you'll have a bit more mental flexibility and awareness to begin to ask those questions. You'll potentially start to see through some of the smoke-and-mirrors, and see into what your future will be at that job. You can begin to interview in a way that they have to impress you instead of the other way around.

That's why I recommend you apply to three jobs a week. Apply to get feedback on your application package, and to practice your interviews in a low-risk way so that when you are more comfortable and capable in the interviewing process, your chances of getting the job you are interested in go up.

Another note about this is that when applying for jobs, you can apply to any position in your field of interest, including the ones that you want. In my experience, applying several times to the same job over a few months has no impact on you as a candidate. As long as you're applying for jobs, you don't have to worry about using up a company or anything like that.

Now that the basic strategy behind applying to jobs three times a week is out of the way, so let's get into the nuts and bolts of applying for jobs!

Job Descriptions

Looking at job postings for the first time is intimidating. It can seem like every job needs a few years of experience before you can apply, and they ask for skills in things you may have never done. The good news is that a lot of job postings are written to be mostly for ideal candidates instead of candidates they'll hire.

Let's look first at years of experience. *My general advice is to take whatever they're asking for and subtract five.* For first-time job hunters, I do recommend applying to any job that has five years or less in the posting.

Years of experience is very misleading as it doesn't correspond to the knowledge or skill they're looking for in a candidate and tends to reflect one of two things. First, it sometimes reflects the experience of the person who left. This case is more common in a specialized or senior role, but if a person who just left the company had been working for four years prior, they might say they expect the same from applicants. This number is unrelated to what they need or will hire. The second case is that years of experience are based more on an impression of how many years of experience a perfect candidate would have.

If you look at a lot of postings, you'll begin to see a common trend in how years of experience tend to be broken down. You'll see a three-to-five set, a five-to-ten, and ten-to-twenty band. That is neat and tidy. Mapping that back to a simplistic grading of developer roles you can quickly see how that first set would be your more entry or junior level, the mid-range could be a middle or senior level, and the last is a wizard.

You'll also notice that at times they'll ask for years of experience using technology that literally hasn't existed that long. Front-end development and JavaScript are particularly prone to this case. Some libraries come and go so quickly that when a posting wants five years of experience with a framework that came out two years ago, something is fishy.

The bottom line is that years of experience aren't hard rules, but mostly exist to represent the idea of a perfect candidate and isn't at all related to the candidate the company will hire or interview. So, take the years of experience, subtract five, and keep going.

Next, I want to talk about titles. More specifically grades of titles. There isn't a standard when it comes to titles in software development. This means that one company's software developer may be another's software engineer. One's junior developer may be another's software engineer. You cannot assume that because a title exists at one company that it exists at others, or means the same thing.

Let me put it another way for you. Junior or entry-level positions are company-specific. If you narrow your search to look for those words, you will miss every company that merely doesn't have a particular junior grade. So by all means, apply to junior positions, but also apply to jobs without those words.

The rule of thumb here is: Apply to postings without "Senior" in the title.

This advice may seem crazy, but it is way too easy to look at a posting and feel that you're not qualified because it doesn't have "Junior" in the title when the company considers a software development title as their junior role. You can't know that from the posting, so if you don't apply, you've missed an opportunity.

Next, when looking at a posting, you'll likely see a standard set of elements. At the top of most postings, you'll see a blurb about the company and position. They'll talk about how amazing the company is and how they're looking for the right person to join their fantastic company at this exact moment. There are great clues here to key into during your research phase, but for now, as long as you don't see a red flag, this content is for fun.

What to Avoid

I want to draw your attention to a few terms to avoid when looking at a job posting for the first time. Thankfully the list is short and even though I steer people away from them, this is more a guide than a rule:

- Rockstar, Ninja, 10x, Cowboy
- Full-Stack
- Start-Up
- Multiple-projects
- Contract

Starting with the rockstar, ninja, 10x, and cowboy thing. These phrases were trendy a little while ago and continue to linger. They are broadly used by companies to describe that they are looking for high-performers and work-a-holics. The language is built to draw out people based on their egos. The reason I tell people to avoid this is that companies that seek out people with egos built around their productivity are likely to be dehumanizing and will burn you out.

Full-stack development jobs are also tricky. You'll tend to see the request for these in smaller companies. I want to be careful with this because you, as a developer, might be competent in a full-stack job. Companies that seek out full-stack developers, however, are usually not responsible enough to have you. The bottom line is that companies seeking full-stack developers are looking for someone who can also do several other jobs at the same time for one salary. You may think that full-stack means back-end and front-end. It may also mean operations, system administration, networking, documentation, production monitoring, and even customer service. Again, there is no guarantee here, but proceed with caution.

Start-ups also get special attention. Start-ups come with a lot of risks. You may join a start-up and wind up unemployed six months later. Working for start-ups require a bit of extra thought and attention to detail if you're going to succeed at one, and you also need to weigh that against what you are genuinely after in this job. Do you want to be around people that help you learn and grow? Do you want stability and benefits? Do you want time to think about how you may best solve a problem? Start-ups may not be able to give you these things.

When working for a start-up, they can be memorable experiences full of passion, late-nights, and people who are singularly devoted to the task at hand. That passion, alignment, and focus are concepts we crave all the time, and start-ups tend to bring it the best. They tend not to have benefits, they tend to compensate with stock instead of salary, and at some point, they all have a do-or-die moment that can be very stressful to survive.

If you want to consider a start-up, weigh the risks against what you're after in a job at this moment.

Last on the list is the phrase, "multiple projects." This phrase is a warning to me. What I see when I read this is that the company will expect me to juggle multiple unrelated projects to completion as though I were only focused on doing one well. These circumstances happen a lot in development agencies. Bouncing between tasks or projects can be very difficult to do without crippling your productivity and making mistakes.

What we're looking for instead is the company that asks that you work on one project until it is complete before moving onto another one. This allows for focus, clarity, and the chance to do great work as you can come back and refine things. When you are forced to juggle multiple projects, the quality tends to be lower, and it can be hard to keep things straight in your head as there is just too much at once.

The last item I listed are contract positions. There are two broad types of contract positions. I'm listing them in this section because these positions aren't for everyone, so I want people to pay attention to this detail so they can make an informed decision.

The first type of contract is called "Contract-to-hire." These positions work off the premise that a company wants to have a trial period with an employee before they convert them to a full-time employee with benefits. There isn't anything wrong with this, but there are a few things that deserve attention. First, whenever you're working on a contract, you generally won't have benefits, time off, and you are responsible for your taxes. So that three-month contract might complicate things for tax season, as well as leave you without health insurance for a few months. These are logistical details to work through, but they may not be things you want to deal with on your first job. Asking your future employer about these items can help.

The next type of contract is an entirely temporary contract position. You'll commonly see these as six- or twelve-month contracts, usually somewhere other than where you are. These are the bread and butter of recruiters whose job it is to find warm bodies.

Again, there isn't anything wrong with these positions. If you can negotiate a high enough rate, don't mind the possibility of moving, and are comfortable with looking for another job near the end of the contract, then go for it. If you're a first-time job-hunter, I don't recommend taking a contract position that requires you to move for your first job. That is a lot of disruption for a temporary contract.

Types of Companies

There are a few main archetypes of companies I want to highlight. While I will paint with a broad brush about companies, there has been, in my experience, enough commonality that it's worth sharing that now. I'm going to cover:

- Agencies and Consultancies
- Start-Ups
- Stable Company
- Sales-Based Company

Agencies and Consultancies

Development agencies and consultancies will tend to have some of the best presentation and ability to market themselves. They'll have a site that talks about how they solve the challenging technical problems for other companies and how they have the best people.

If you're unsure if you're applying to one, I recommend paying attention to their main page. When you look into what they do, if their purpose is to solve another company's problem in software development, you've found an agency or consultancy. They may say it outright in their other material, but sometimes it isn't apparent.

You may be asking what the difference between a consultancy or agency is, but in practicality, there isn't one. Now, people who are proud to work for consultancies may get angry at this, but for the sake of this book, it isn't a distinction worth making.

These companies continuously need an influx of new developers and will often be the most eager to hire people. It is an essential aspect of their business model. They operate by placing their development staff on client projects where developers work on the projects while billing forty hours a week. Some of these consultancies require travel, and some do not. Some need you to be on the client site, and some do not.

Agencies and consultancies highly value developers that can work seamlessly with clients. If you have any past experience working directly with clients, this will help you stand out. The downside to agencies and consultancies is that they can be stressful and frantic. When the client contract is coming to an end, or trust has eroded with the client, you may begin to see the stress. These circumstances breed a decaying work environment that often causes people to quit. Many consultancies and agencies have some of the highest turnover in the industry for this reason.

Consultancies will regularly pay above market value, while agencies will remain competitive.

Start-Ups

I mentioned a bit about start-ups above, but these companies are all about generating customers, revenue, and traction. It's an all-hands-on-deck, all-the-time life. It can be a thrill with a terrible crash at the end and is wildly unpredictable. Generally, salaries will be lower, benefits worse or non-existent, but with generous stock options. These variables change depending on what stage of growth and investment the start-up is in.

I mentioned before how it can be enjoyable to work in a company where everyone is completely aligned, focused, and working hard together toward the same things. It is exciting to work in a company where the CEO is a few feet from you and wants to know what you think. It is one of the few times when a software developer has the chance to change the future of a company entirely.

The risks are enormous at a start-up. They may never make a profit or revenue, and their funding may run out. That big bet that everyone stayed up late at night shipping may be a flop. Things can change very quickly at a start-up. If you're looking for stability, this won't be for you. Everyone is going to be doing their best to make the company succeed. The name of the game is to ship quickly. This time in a company's life doesn't often leave a lot of room for a culture of growth and mentoring. In other words, you may need help, and everyone will be too busy to help.

Stable Company

Next, we come to our more stable companies. These will pay competitively for the market, offer benefits, and stability. You'll be a developer put into a team within a department with layers of management working on a project for months or years. It can be challenging to know what the point of your work is. You may come and go before anything you built goes to market. Things can move very slowly in these companies.

In spite of that, you get stability. You also can enjoy a slower and more relaxed pace most of the time. People are encouraged to help one another. Senior engineers will be expected to help newer ones. Stable companies often have an environment where the work may not be satisfactory, but the opportunity to learn exists in a more structured way. A downside is that many people who work in companies like this feel like a cog in a machine. You may never see the CEO.

Sales-Based Company

Lastly, a sales-based company may be hard to spot. The best clues will be found in the staff rosters and other open positions. If you see a lot of sales, vice-presidents, or growth positions, you have a strong clue. If the material on their site talks about growing business or revenue, that's a good clue.

Sales companies are notorious for highs and lows. One minute you might be working on an important project, and within minutes you'll be called into an urgent meeting because the development team must ship some proof-of-concept or a new feature right now or they lose a deal. These companies pay competitively, their benefits can be good or minimal, and stability is questionable. While the sales group sells, things will be great, but in leaner times they'll let people go. You may also wind up signing more aggressive paperwork when joining a company that is shaped by sales.

The upshot of working at a sales company is that you'll be able to know a lot about the customers you're there to serve through your software. You'll know because the sales group will talk about it all the time. This level of connectedness is deeply satisfying for many developers. The downside is the whiplash that comes in a company like this, which tends to leave the software of abject and fractured quality. When one salesperson needs a new feature for one client, that request turns into an emergency project for the development teams. The next salesperson needs another custom change for their client. Suddenly the product codebase is littered with small unique features that nobody can remember but have to stay there. Technical excellence can be a challenge in a sales company.

With all these broad statements, the size of the company will change a lot of these variables. Smaller companies will have more extremes with less compensation. Medium companies will have a reasonable amount of stability and salary. Large companies will have so much security that people may never even realize you work there, and the compensation will be fair as well. So you can look at a company from two angles, the first is the size, and the second is the type of company. These angles can give clues as to what you might expect.

Where to Look

Over the years, there have been numerous sites that claim to help job-hunters find their perfect job. The ones that are the most effective change every year, so let's talk about which ones seem to be the most useful in 2020.

The job-help sites I'll cover here are:

- StackOverflow[10]
- LinkedIn[11]
- Glassdoor[12]
- Recruiters
- Your contacts!

This list is by no means comprehensive, but these few stand out among all of the other sources. These sites are not overrun with recruiters spamming everyone with positions. You may be wondering why I have recruiters on my list while also saying many of the sites also aren't about recruiters. That is because the jobs that many recruiters post are of low quality or so poorly written that they are a pain to deal with and sift through. Also, working with recruiters is different than applying to a recruiter.

Let's take a look at StackOverflow[13]. If this is the first time you've heard of this site, it's a tool most commonly used for software

---

[10]https://stackoverflow.com
[11]https://linkedin.com
[12]https://glassdoor.com
[13]https://stackoverflow.com

development. When a developer has a question, more than likely someone on StackOverflow has answered it. What you may not know is that they have a careers site. This site tends to offer some of the highest-quality positions that you'll find in terms of the fewest red-flags. They also have a few unique ways of categorizing jobs based on technical practices and remote friendliness. This categorization means that the person submitting the posting has to know a few things before they send the position. That raises the bar for the postings you'll find there.

LinkedIn[14] is next on the list, but not because of its quality. LinkedIn has the most recruiter job postings on the list, but it is paired nicely with company information and your professional network. That means that you can search for jobs based on people you know and trust. You can make contact with people within these companies through your contacts. Those connections drastically improve your chances of getting hired. We'll talk a bit more about using your network to get jobs a bit later.

Glassdoor[15] is a new player in the space of company sites. I'll mention it again in the research section. Similar to LinkedIn, you can search for jobs based on your standard location and title criteria, and the postings aren't all recruiter spam. What makes Glassdoor so lovely is the type of research it can give while you research the job. You can look at a posting right alongside the salary history of people who took that same position. You can read reviews of the company from employees and get an impression of what things may be like inside the company.

Next up are recruiters. *Recruiters* have their own chapter, but for the sake of applying for jobs I'll say this: They provide opportunities with companies that you may never know about otherwise. Many companies only work through recruiting agencies for their hiring. That means the only way to get in is through a recruiter. Even though there is a chapter on dealing with recruiters which I

---

[14]https://linkedin.com
[15]https://glassdoor.com

recommend you read before engaging with them, for now, think of them as people who can give you even more opportunities.

Last, and most importantly are the people you know. I might best phrase that as people you've met. Your contacts, no matter how much or little you know them, can tell you not only about the jobs their company has, but also what jobs will be coming up soon. I've never worked for a company that went through the effort of making a posting public if they already found a candidate. Also, even if your contact doesn't have anything at their place, they may know someone whose company is hiring and introduce you. As you hang out in the industry, you'll find out it is a lot smaller than you realize, and that the people you know will help you stay employed and avoid the bad companies too.

Now that we've covered the places, I want to spend a moment connecting this back to the strategy of applying to three jobs a week. For the websites, this is a straightforward process of going to the sites, looking at what some of your saved searches show, and applying to the jobs that make sense. If you're lucky, you won't wind up having to go through an obnoxious online application process that takes forever, but either way, you'll get good at those in time too. For recruiters, once you engage with one, they'll begin to call you every week or two with opportunities. You'll have to listen to what they're offering as they don't know what is appropriate, but applying through them counts as one of your three. Last, if you're going to leverage your contacts, begin to reach out and find those positions through the people you've met.

The game here is to apply to three jobs a week. The places I've listed offer high-quality jobs as well, which makes this a little easier.

There may be other sites you've wondered about as well, some of those might be:

- Monster
- Indeed

- Dice

These sites used to be the best out there, but over time lost their quality to recruiters filling the sites up with everything instead of jobs of reasonable quality. I list them here as they are an easy way to find even more jobs, but more than likely it will help you find a recruiter.

Research

Once you've chosen the job to apply to, you will need to do some research on them. The reason you'll do research is to adjust your resume and cover letter appropriately. You can skip all of this, but it hurts your chances. You will, however, need to do this before an interview.

When researching to apply for the job, I recommend looking in just a few places. Again, you'll want to make a few tweaks to your resume and cover letter to tailor them to the company. The amount of information you need to do that is less than you may think.

To prepare your application, I want you to look at:

- The job description
- The main website
- The careers page
- The about page
- The company news

Most of the information you can leverage will come straight out of the job description. Within the job post, you'll know the skills they want you to emphasize in your resume and cover letter. Often at the top of the posting, they'll have a paragraph or two about the company and the project or initiative. These paragraphs are great information to weave back into your cover letter or resume experience to show how you're a perfect fit for that need.

On the main website, you will get a better feel for the company itself. Sometimes you'll find that the job posting and the company website don't seem to line up. As confusing as that may be, it's good to know now that there may be either specific types of dysfunction internally with communication or that the business is complex enough that you may not be able to make sense of it. I felt that way when working at an advertising company.

On the careers page, they'll likely espouse their excellent work culture and values. This page is a gold-mine for information to place into your cover letter. Showing how you're a person with the same values and that you fit into their culture already makes you a natural choice for anyone sifting through applications. It also can give you a few specific details that you can use to ask questions in the interview process. Maybe you see something about company lunches that you want to know more about, or that they have training budgets for their employees. These are great things to ask about because they can be great perks, and they show how engaged you are as a candidate.

The about page for a company will tell the company's history. Some things I look for here are if the company had a different business model in the past, if they've changed leadership recently, and then between all the writing what the real story of this company is. Sometimes I get the impression that under all of the polished language, this company is all about making money and the events of its past were moments on that timeline. Maybe you see that their company story is only about investment and never about a customer, or that it is about shareholders and not customers or employees. Do the values on the about page line up with the ones on the careers page?

Lastly, I take a quick look at news about the company. There may be recent events that you can make commentary about in your cover letter and also ask questions about in your interview. I was recently at a company, and I asked about their recent acquisition. That question led to a two-hour conversation about what that experience was like for them. This story may seem like a pointless anecdote, but in my experience, if your interviews turn conversational and they're doing a lot of the talking, the interview is going well.

When getting ready to apply, I will quickly flip through these materials. Each takes no more than two minutes or so. For each one, I'm looking for things I can weave into my resume and cover letter. I'm looking for questions I can ask during the interview, and for inconsistencies that I may want to keep in the back of my mind if I decide to consider an offer.

Since you're applying for three of these in a week, I also recommend taking notes about each job where you send an application. You don't have to be thorough, but a date you applied, if you did any major experiments with your application package, and any impressions you had of them during your research. That way, if they call you up next month, you won't be starting completely over, or if you wind up with three companies to interview with, you will have some notes to keep it straight.

The Best Way to Apply

For the first-timers, this section's advice comes in when you're getting interviews regularly, and you suspect you're going to get offers soon. This section is about your best chance of getting an interview.

The best way to apply to a job is through your contacts.

It may feel a little gross to reach out to people and ask if their company is hiring, but you'll want to get over that feeling quickly.

Fifty-two percent[16] of all hires come from recommendations.

There are a few things that happen when asking your contacts about jobs. First, if it is within their own company, they are unlikely to recommend you join them if they hate the job themselves. So, your contacts will serve as a natural filter for bad situations. They won't be perfect, but they're on the ground there every day, so they have an excellent idea of what the place is like and can help you understand that.

Also, when they refer you, more than likely, they will get a referral bonus. Many companies offer a bonus that ranges from a few hundred to a few thousand dollars for someone they hire. I've made a bit of extra money doing this in my time. So, if you're feeling gross after that, remember, your request may get them paid.

Lastly, when someone within a company puts your resume on HR's desk, it gets a stamp of approval. Instead of someone trying to see if your material goes in the yes pile, the attitude changes. You're already going to get a pass unless they find something that sets off an alarm. Another way to look at it is that you have to give them a reason to say no to you. That happens for the same reason that many people won't recommend you work with them if they hate their job, companies trust that if their employee puts a resume forward that they, on some level, endorse them.

Now, when going down this path, I recommend a few things. First, ask everyone you've ever met. It doesn't matter how close you are, but you may want to start with people you can stand to feel awkward with as you do this the first few times. As you get more comfortable, expand who you approach. You're looking for work with them, or if they know someone who might. Keep asking. Take your request online! My Twitter feed is full every day of people who are helping near-strangers connect in their network of people.

---

[16]Maurer, Roy. "Employee Referrals Remain Top Source for Hires" SHRM. https://www.shrm.org/resourcesandtools/hr-topics/talent-acquisition/pages/employee-referrals-remains-top-source-hires.aspx (accessed December 26, 2019)

Next, if it seems like there is a lead to be had, give them your resume. This step may sound obvious, but it isn't to a lot of people, including the person who is helping you. You want them to have the resume because when they have your resume, it compels them to actually refer you. Everyone is busy, so it is easy for people to get distracted with their day-to-day stuff, but when they keep seeing your resume in front of them, they know they need to refer you. Second, some companies require the person to submit your info themselves to get credit. This requirement is the detail many people don't quite know if they haven't done it before. When it comes to giving them your resume, they may push back, but you do want to find a way to put it in their hands.

Last, you may need to pester your contacts a bit. I wrote above how easy it is to get distracted with day-to-day work. Every day they're distracted is a day that you don't have that job. Find a way to politely nudge them to refer you in. Pestering becomes increasingly important when trying to get an introduction to someone else that may have a job. If you find yourself in that situation, try to get the introduction immediately together. You can also write an introduction for them to make it easy. The point is that you don't want your potential job to fall into jeopardy because your contacts get distracted.

Consider taking them out for coffee or a beer to catch up and hear more about the job. Pull out your laptop and see if you can write the introduction together, or send your resume in together. One of the people I mentored was masterful at inviting people out to beers to catch up, and then a few days later he'd be interviewing for their company. Find your way and style to leverage your contacts to get your resume in.

7 - Recruiters

At some point in the job-hunting process, you'll wind up encountering a recruiter. They may already send you emails or requests through social networking. They are everywhere and are an essential part of the job search for software developers.

I take a pretty strong view on recruiters, and that will come through in this chapter, but I see recruiters as people who have access to jobs that are otherwise inaccessible through other means. So, learning to work with them will be key to getting access to more opportunities.

Recruiter Services

A recruiter exists to connect companies with viable candidates. When recruiters place a candidate, they get paid. One figure I heard was that they are paid up to thirty percent of the candidate's salary. That is a hefty fee!

In practical terms, it means that recruiters are scouring social media, internal databases, conferences, meet-ups, and contacts to find eager job-hunters that they can place into jobs. One way you'll meet them is through their ability to find and reach out to you, but another way is that you apply to a job and find out that you've applied to a recruiter's posting. Either way, you'll find one another.

From there, they will set up your profile with your resume and whatnot and then tell you about various positions they have in their portfolio. If you decide to apply, they'll put your material into a lovely packet and send it to their client on your behalf. Should the company choose to interview you, the recruiter may or may not help you prepare, but they will coordinate the interview schedule for you. From this point forward, the recruiter will help with communication and apply pressure on the company to move quickly with you. After all, they want this to wrap up, and people in companies have other jobs and are quickly distracted. Their ability to chase things down and keep the process moving is one of my favorite qualities of recruiters. They can turn a month-long process into one that takes a week.

After that, they'll ensure you get the offer, and it is signed. From there you may see that recruiter again for a quick follow-up, and they'll likely contact you again with future jobs or for contacts.

All said, the two greatest assets a recruiter brings is their portfolio of jobs and their ability to push the process through to completion. The rest of what they bring may come with a few interesting side-effects to deal with.

Working with Recruiters

When it comes to working effectively with recruiters, there are a few things I think every job-seeker should know. For the first-time job hunters, you can treat what I'm about to describe as informational. As you gain more experience and have a clearer direction in your career, you will likely want to change the parameters of how you engage a recruiter.

The first thing I want you to realize about recruiters is that they aren't technical people and generally have almost no knowledge about the job itself. So, when they call you about positions, you'll likely find out very quickly that they are listing jobs that you have no qualifications for at all. That is because they don't know, and they're hoping that by casting a broader net you'll surprise them by wanting to go for a job that may seem like a stretch. So the first thing to pay attention to is the job they're describing. You'll have to be the one that says yes or no to those jobs. This decision is one you can't responsibly leave to a recruiter. They don't know.

I'd like for you to be aware that many recruiters will take your resume and make some adjustments on your behalf. These adjustments range from putting your resume into a standard format on their stationary, to re-ordering your experience, to outright editing your experience. In my decade of doing this, only one recruiter ever asked permission before making changes. So, even though the recruiter will create a packet for their client, you might find yourself slightly misrepresented without realizing it. Now, you may get an interview from it, but who knows what they saw in your resume.

I worked with one recruiter and wound up getting a job through them. After a few months with the company, I was interviewing people as well. The hiring manager kept all the packets in a folder, and as I was looking at the candidate's package, I thumbed through the pile of packets and found my own. The recruiter had reformatted my resume and chopped off around three years of experience to make it fit on one page. After I completed the interview, I printed my actual resume and placed them side-by-side on the desk of the manager. They were shocked this was happening. It didn't result in terminating the recruiting agency, but it did serve as an educational moment for the company to realize that they were being served doctored resumes for candidates.

Next, and this one is a little tricky, is that once you engage with a recruiter for a job, you have also often agreed to let the recruiter represent you with that company. You'll need to check what agreements you sign when working with them, but if a recruiter tells you about a position, and then you apply behind their back, you might have violated a contract. At the very least, the recruiter will know this happened, and since they very likely have a positive relationship with that company, a word from them could greatly diminish your chances of getting hired.

Now, this doesn't mean that you can't keep applying to jobs outside of what the recruiter has told you. It means that, depending on what you've agreed to, if a recruiter tells you about a position you may need to work with them throughout your application with that particular company.

Another possibility is that the recruiter will likely route all communication through themselves. You may not even realize this happens. While I can't say for sure what the intent is, I believe it is to ensure that the recruiter only allows the kinds of communication that give you your best chances. They'll prevent half-baked emails from going through, rephrase things, and so-on. This filtering isn't always a problem, but if you find that you need to get answers while working on a technical assignment or negotiate your offer, then this becomes an issue. It can be tough to get the clarification you need or set the right expectations with a company if the recruiter is handling your communication. It can be nearly impossible to negotiate if the recruiter is between you and them. Setting clear parameters with your recruiter at the onset is the best way to go. Sometimes I tell them that I'll run things by them first, but I need direct access with the hiring company. Getting a recruiter to remove themselves as a communication gatekeeper is difficult.

One of the recruiter's best traits is that they'll chase down the company to keep things moving. You'd be amazed at how many times you start applying for a job only to find that the manager goes on vacation as soon as you begin the process. The recruiter will try to find other people to interview you instead of waiting a week. The company may also have some critical release that has everyone's attention, but the recruiter will keep pushing on them to find a way to interview you. They won't stop until they get what they want, and that means a quick interview process for you. Without a recruiter, you often have no real contact with people within a company to figure out where things are in terms of scheduling your interview.

Another benefit that recruiters offer is that you can ask them what feedback the company had about you. This feedback is invaluable when a recruiter can get it. Be warned though, often the feedback is pretty bland and may not offer much detail. Either way, some feedback is better than none in this case. Because a recruiter exists as this somewhat neutral third party with a relationship with both parties, they can act as a go-between and search out what people thought of you. Companies are happy to provide recruiters with feedback because it means the recruiter can use it to find different candidates as well. You can use this to find out more about how well you're interviewing and presenting yourself as a candidate.

Lastly, recruiters often are the ones who will communicate with the company about your salary. If you give a recruiter your salary history, they will provide it to the company. Your history will be the input they use to inform your offer. The recruiter may also give insight to you as to what the probable compensation is for the position as they've likely placed people before. The challenge here is that you have no say in your salary at this point. The recruiter and company will find a number and then give it to you. The recruiter will almost always tell you to accept it and will never want you to negotiate. Negotiation has risk, so why invite that risk when you have an offer in hand? So, if you expect a recruiter to get you the best compensation available, think again. They want you to get a fair offer, but they aren't going to ask for ten percent more for you when they believe they have a reasonable offer.

To counter this last point, I set clear parameters with the recruiter about salary and negotiation. They will often insist that they need my salary history or target to present me to a company. I flatly refuse to talk about salary with them. I go further to say that I will be negotiating my salary and that I insist that the recruiter not discuss my compensation with the company. I say this firmly, and I don't waiver regardless of the objections I hear.

One recruiter was particularly obstinate about wanting to discuss salary on my behalf and preventing me from negotiating. I offered a deal to the recruiter. I said that they could negotiate my salary if I can be their recruiter and arrange their next salary too. The bottom line is that I can negotiate a higher salary almost every job I get, but by allowing a recruiter to settle, I could be giving up over ten thousand dollars a year. That price, to me, makes the confrontation worthwhile.

Bottom-Line

Recruiters are an interesting group to deal with, but critical in the job hunt. They have access to jobs that nobody else does, and they can get you interviewed quickly. Know the consequences of how they operate in terms of altering resumes, owning the communication, and setting up your salary. For the first-timer, don't worry about these things and focus on interviewing and getting the offer. For your second job onward, consider setting clear boundaries and parameters with your recruiter so that you have the best chances of getting the best offer that you can.

8 - Interviewing Strategy

If you're reading this chapter, I'm going to assume a few things. One is that you're starting to get interviews, or you're interested in preparing for them. If you're following the plan I outlined I'm going to assume the strategy is working, and you're on your way to the success of getting interviews.

You may also read this chapter because this isn't your first time through the process, and you're looking for some new tips and tricks to help you through it. I aim to give you exactly that during this chapter.

The reality is that interviews are the most stressful part of job-hunting. Interviewing is the tipping point where companies have decided you have potential, but now want you to show it. Many people are not trained or taught to conduct interviews professionally. Which, on the one hand, means you have to deal with some interviews that set you up to fail and, on the other, is an opportunity for you to exploit the situation for your own benefit.

I sometimes describe interviewing as a game. You are one player, and your employer and their interviewers are your opponents. The rules may be vague, but there are numerous openings and opportunities to win this game, even if it seems like the game favors them instead.

I hope that through this book, the dynamic shifts in favor of the skillful candidate. Until companies invest in training their employees on better, more human-centric approaches to hiring, the benefit is that you'll be more skilled at getting a job while that happens, and when companies do finally figure this out, you'll be highly experienced and earn a higher band of compensation.

Someone I mentor told me the story of a recent interview. My pupil did her research and formed the impression that this company valued hobbies and personal growth in their employees. For her remote interview, she staged her room to show off elements of her hobbies to draw the interviewers in. It worked masterfully, and she was able to immediately bring them into her story, simply by placing a few well-chosen items in the room.

Making the Right First Impression

There are a lot of strange rules about interviews that are going out of date, but they mostly pertain to making the right first impression. I'll write my personal opinion about how best to do this, but you can form your own opinion about this advice.

Before I landed my first development job, I was a bartender. Chatting with the regulars about how I was looking to get into my career soon, we talked about what it was like for their first jobs and how important it was to make the right first impression. One man told this story from his younger days.

When a candidate wanted to come work for his company, they'd be invited out to lunch at a favorite steakhouse. This lunch was the interview, but the candidate had no idea. The interviewers were watching who this person was the entire meal and would decide if they moved on or not based on their behavior. One candidate, they told me, ordered a steak and proceeded to put salt on it before his first bite. He didn't get the job.

I was astounded and asked how they could make such a decision from something like table salt. The justification was that the candidate decided he knew what was best for the steak without even trying what a professional had provided. That kind of attitude was bound to spell trouble at the job if he was going to go around pretending he knew best before ever trying things the way they had developed them first.

That story is from decades ago so I wouldn't worry about its impact on your interviews today. There are certainly plenty of weird things that go on in interviews, but I'm willing to recommend that you don't need to worry about table salt.

What are the key elements that I think lead to a good first impression? Well, I think it's worthwhile describing a few key things:

- Appearance
- Confidence
- Composure
- Eye-contact
- Day-of planning

Appearance

Admittedly, this one is a bit variable depending on the industry, so doing your homework ahead of time will help. Generally speaking, the software industry moved away from any notion of business attire during interviews some time ago.

If you are applying to a job whose specialty or core business is not software, then dress the way people do for their main line of business. For example, if you're going into a bank, dress like the banking industry does. If you're going into a start-up, dress like you're not homeless yet.

Aside from clothing, tailor your appearance so that you will minimally not offend and optimally charm. Present yourself in a way that makes it look like you've got your life together.

During my senior year at my university, we had to take a class called Senior Design. We were divided into teams and then farmed out to local companies to build small projects as interns. Throughout the course, we took personality tests and talked about what it means to work with people different than ourselves. We had a whole book about working with other people. One chapter I remember even over a decade later: Hygiene. Not in the context of interviewing for jobs, but for on the job. It had wisdom in it like using soap, deodorant, and brushing your teeth. It had more advanced topics like using mouthwash after a particularly funky meal if you'll be working closely with people afterward.

I wish I could say that this chapter wasn't needed, but at my university it was. The good news is that out in the professional world, this will likely never matter, but this story is an absurd way to highlight that if you haven't given any thought to your appearance, I'd recommend you reconsider. Now that we're past the basics, there are a few other things I want to bring up.

Getting a good night's sleep is important for a lot of reasons, but in terms of your appearance, it'll prevent you from looking like the undead during your interview. Looking tired or sleepy can rub people the wrong way, and it isn't something you can caffeinate away.

Also, there is some old advice that I'm going to retain. Bring a pen and a pad of paper. You never have to write in it. I rarely do. It does, however, show that you're prepared to engage in the interview, and I've heard enough people complain about candidates over the years who didn't bring anything that I will pass this advice forward. As much as it matters to be prepared, you need to look prepared.

Confidence

While I advocate bringing who you are, completely and wholly to an interview, I also advise that you do so with confidence. Confidence has an intoxicating effect in an interview.

There was a notable TED Talk[17] by Amy Cuddy where the presenter

---

[17]Cuddy, Amy. "Your Body Language May Shape Who You Are" TED.com. https://www.ted.com/talks/amy_cuddy_your_body_language_shapes_who_you_are (accessed December 26, 2019)

described several experiments where people were asked to watch interviews and then describe the candidates.

Some of the candidates were given specific coaching to be confident and others were not. The ones that acted confident were the same candidates the panel chose over and over. In other words, confidence alone improves your chances.

The coached candidates were instructed to go to the bathroom and stand in a superhero pose for two minutes. The pose works by spreading your legs about shoulder-width apart, placing your hands on your hips, and puffing your chest out. Imagine Wonder Woman or Superman standing there. Do this in front of a mirror and look at yourself in that pose. The two minutes is enough to trick your brain temporarily into believing that it is in control, which will lead to you appearing more confident.

How does it look to be confident? Well, if you look into body language, you'll find the concepts of closed or open body language. Taking up lots of space and leaving your vulnerable spots exposed are characterizations of open body language. Imagine sitting across from a hungry lion. Open body language would be shown by someone who isn't afraid of the lion and therefore, may not protect their vital areas. They would sit or lounge as if they own the place during an interview. Some examples would be to lean back in a chair, arms laid across chair backs or an upright posture.

Closed body language, in contrast, is when the body tends to collapse inward. Going back to the lion metaphor, closed language would have the person balling up to protect themselves. This kind of language demonstrates fear, anxiety, and uncertainty. Examples are sitting with knees together, slouching forward, or crossing arms. Closed body language, even in a highly competent person, can leave an interviewer with uncertainty about the candidate. The impression of uncertainty comes from the closed body language.

In the end, we want to find ways to feel confident in our interviews as they show strength, certainty, courage, and fearlessness. These impressions easily substitute for competence. Consider the level of confidence you show in an interview as another variable that you can control for, increasing your chances for hire.

I often tell people that the best time to interview is when you are employed. The reason is that it affords a low-risk situation, and you walk into the interview with very little to lose, which helps improve confidence. The extra confidence, in turn, leaves a stronger impression that leads to a higher chance of getting an offer. When you don't have a job or are desperate for one, you tend to be less confident, either because you're not sure if you'll get the job you need, or because you doubt your abilities. This uncertainty shows up as closed body language, which then communicates that you're uncertain, which then casts doubt as to your competence.

Having said all of that, I'm not advocating being an egotistical jerk. I'm supporting a sense of assurance within yourself. I don't recommend walking into an interview and expressing confidence by bragging about how you're the greatest thing ever. I'm looking for you to walk into the room knowing that you have worth, that you will succeed in showing it, and that there is another job waiting for you too. This attitude is healthy confidence where you are likely to be in your best frame of mind while also showing the kind of self-assurance that leads to a favorable impression.

If you think this is all crazy, try the superhero pose one day and see if people regard you at all differently afterward. More than likely you will feel like things went better for you, and if you can get quality feedback from someone, they may confirm it even if they're unable to pinpoint what it was that made you seem more put together at the time.

Composure

Closely related to confidence is composure. I highlight its importance separately because at some point in the interviewing process, especially if you are new to it, you are likely to get rattled. In fact, I would say that many interviews are designed to do just that.

Finding ways to maintain a cool head and keep the panic at bay is very important to navigating interviews. I want you to think of the most recent moment you felt like you were losing your calm. How did that affect your line of thinking? What happened to cause that moment? How did you recover? These questions, if you've never considered them, may help you uncover more about who you are and what kinds of circumstances put you into a frame of mind that isn't ideal for interviews.

If I were to say that calm and composed is our ideal state, then panic would be the opposite. During an interview, every moment is a test. If you reach a point of fear, the chances of you making a mistake skyrocket. It may not be anything so bad as giving a wrong answer, but it could be that you answer poorly. What I mean is that when you feel like you're moving away from calm and toward panic, your voice may change, your answers may get short, your tone may become more hostile, you may inadvertently show your frustration on your face. While none of these things mean that you don't get the job, you are not the only person interviewing. If your competition maintains their composure better, they'll look better.

Unfortunately, I can't say, "Be calm," and consider that sorted. People don't come with a dial we can use to turn the calm on when we want to. Composure is born out of awareness of oneself and what circumstances jeopardize that calm. A likely set of events that may knock you off balance are:

- Answering a question you don't have an answer to
- Solving a problem you don't understand
- Solving a problem with an absurd set of constraints
- Answering questions that get very close to being personal
- Answering questions that you know are trick questions
- Answering the same question numerous times

- Meeting people, learning their names, and interacting with them in a matter of minutes

I am an introvert, so almost all social interaction has the potential to knock me off balance. I'm cutting the list off here because it highlights several circumstances that cause people some degree of panic.

The good news is that the plan I outlined in *The Plan* is specifically designed to address these issues. I want you applying to three jobs a week so you get plenty of interviews as practice before you target the job you want. One primary reason for that recommendation is to get real experience with the circumstances that cause you to lose your composure in an interview. You will have numerous chances to gather your awareness of how you respond to the interview process, and you'll be able to find ways to balance yourself.

The most dreaded example I know of is whiteboarding. I'll describe that process in depth in *The Interview Stages*, but that practice is designed to put the candidate out of their comfort zone and perform while being judged. I've never met a developer who experienced anything other than dread during this experience. Over the years, those of us that had to whiteboard learned to remain composed through them. We learned to cope with the absurdity of it. Many developers have normalized its absurdity to the point that they believe it is a valid way to test competency.

It isn't.

The point is that the process I outlined will have you going into numerous interviews where you'll experience whiteboarding and other instances that cause you to lose your composure. Because you'll have so many chances to do it, you'll find ways to get your calmness back, develop strategies to cope with the circumstances, and practice excelling at them. Some of these things you can practice at home, but I believe that practicing at home will only carry you so far. At some point, you will have to do this for a real interview, and you can't predict what will happen.

I have a friend who took Karate for years. I remember going to watch his training one evening, and they were sparring that night. My friend got up in front of his instructor and, for the first time, I saw my friend scared. He had the techniques and muscle memory all down, so he stood in good form, he knew how to act, but he was terrified of getting hit. He lost his composure, and that destroyed his ability to spar. His instructor realized this and stopped sparring. He told my friend to lean in so he could punch him in the face. My friend was mortified at the thought, but his instructor pointed out that if he got hit in the face now, he'd have a lot less to be afraid of when sparring, and maybe he'd have a chance.

By interviewing over and over, you'll get the same punch to the face. You'll be able to keep your composure as you acclimate to the experience of interviewing and you'll be able to maintain your balance far better.

Eye-Contact

In the vein of confidence, I also want to take a little time to address something which is still challenging for me. When interviewing, making clear eye-contact helps to quickly establish a better rapport and relationship.

I say that I struggle with it because I find making eye-contact too confrontational. I can do it for short amounts of time or if I genuinely prepare myself mentally ahead of time. However, the effort I put into eye-contact pays off in having people engage with me more deeply and personally in all circumstances of life, and that includes interviews.

What I try to do at a minimum is make eye-contact during a few particular times. The first is when I'm introducing myself to others. I am intentional about making a good first impression during the 'handshake moment' by having clear eye-contact with people during the entire introduction. The second is when someone, myself included, is leaving the room. I consider that I can cement my good impression on them as we go our separate ways. I want them to remember me, so I make eye-contact at the end as well.

Beyond those two moments, I try throughout my interview to make eye-contact whenever I want to drive a point home to my interviewers. So, if I'm sharing a story from my past and I want to emphasize a specific strength or that I took an imperfect but pragmatic approach, I will make eye contact as I make that particular point.

If eye-contact can deepen a relationship, then it seems to me that doing so at strategic moments when I am trying to tell them about my qualities makes sense.

Aside from those moments, my ability to make eye-contact is tied to energy levels and what the focus is. Many in-person interviews are like a marathon. They can last for hours without any significant breaks, but everything you do is judged. It can be exhausting. Combine that with having to answer questions that may require all of my attention, and I don't have the capacity to make eye-contact the whole time. When I realize this is true, I focus on those few key moments.

Contrasting tactical or solid eye-contact with almost none may also be helpful. If, as an interviewer, I interview someone who never once looks me in the eye, I may question their honesty or think something is wrong. The phrase that might get used when reviewing the candidate would be that they can't give a straight answer. Now, this impression can happen through lack of eye-contact as much as it can through the choice of words within the candidate's response. With occasional eye-contact, I'll feel like they are direct and honest. Each of these is desirable traits.

Day-of Planning

Scheduling and conducting interviews can be a bit of a logistical nightmare. If currently employed at a job, you'll have to work around time off. If you are already at a software job, you may do all of this secretly and need excuses to throw people off.

When You Already Have a Job

Before moving on, I want to talk a little bit about when you're at a software job and you're looking at another one. Every company will tell you that they want to know if you're looking for something else so that they can help you. This sentiment is lovely but is rarely backed up in practice.

The reality is that once your company finds out or believes that you're leaving, they may begin to isolate you. You may find that you aren't invited to meetings over time. The work you're allowed to take on becomes trivial, and you have to spend time either teaching someone else or documenting what you know. By the end of two weeks, you'll be sitting at your desk twiddling your thumbs. Companies don't mean anything ill by doing this. They are managing risk.

During your time at the company, you will undoubtedly have gained a significant amount of expertise in their systems and code and current projects. If the company does nothing, they put themselves in danger of having a considerable disruption when your expertise vanishes with your new job. I'm not suggesting that when companies do this, they're doing something well. I'm only telling you what they are doing.

Keep in mind that there is no prerequisite that you have an offer. All they need is to think you're looking and they may put this plan into action. What happens when they've isolated you, and you don't have a job? How long will they let you sit doing nothing? Even if it was their design to make you useless, how long will they pay you?

You might inadvertently wind up out of a job before you ever got an offer for another one.

Having seen this scenario played out time after time, I'm forced to give this advice: *Don't tell your employer anything until you have a signed offer.*

In reality, you aren't likely obligated to tell them anything. In at-will states, you aren't even required to give notice. So, unless you live in a state with other laws, or you have signed something compelling you to do differently, say nothing. Don't tell co-workers. They'll talk, and word will spread. Then the company will believe you're looking.

If this is you, you'll want to employ stealth to navigate this, but even if that isn't true and you're working at a non-software job, the same logistical hurdles exist. You'll need to schedule your interviews around the time you have available and the time off you can get.

I once conducted two hours of interviews in my car in the neighboring office's parking lot. I didn't have a lot of vacation to use, so I took the interviews over lunch and said I had an appointment for the other hour. You can figure out a way to navigate these logistical hurdles.

The Day Of the Interviews

Let's change gears and talk about the day of your interviews. Often these will last a few hours and have you interviewing with multiple people back-to-back. You may even wind up answering the same questions over and over. Either way, you'll be in a room for a few hours, interviewing. There are things you can do to plan for this too.

First, before going in, ask for some water. You may not be thirsty now, but you will be after speaking non-stop for over an hour. Then, find out where the toilets are. Most of the time, you'll be escorted in by someone from HR who will also be one of the last people you see.

During the majority of the interview, however, various people will come and go to interview you. You can certainly ask them where the restrooms are, but having it mapped out ahead is one less detail.

Have breath mints out of sight, but nearby.

Think ahead in terms of what you'll eat leading up to your interview. Since you want to look good, think twice before eating something full of sauce or grease that can mess up your clothes. Also, take into consideration how you will feel after that particular meal. Avoid foods that you know make you feel nauseous, gassy, uncomfortable, or gross. Eat food that makes you either feel good or nothing at all.

Imagine being in an interview after a large soda, trying to keep your belches away and having to go to the bathroom while not knowing where it is. You won't be at your best during that interview.

My advice around planning even to the point of the food you consume may sound obsessive, but every variable you account for can lead to higher chances of success. I love eating buffalo wings, and I'd happily eat them anytime. I wouldn't dare eat them before an interview. I know I'd likely stain my clothes and fingers. I don't want to smell like buffalo sauce either. I'll delay that gratification until another time.

If you wind up realizing that your interview is around lunch, recognize that this means you won't get to eat lunch unless you eat before or after. Some companies will take you out to lunch, but they'll likely tell you that as you schedule things. You might think, how could they schedule me during lunch and not feed me? Well, since everyone is coming and going, everyone else gets to eat around their small block of time with you. You are the only one in a room for hours. Plan ahead if this is your scenario.

In between your interviews, stand up and move around if you've been sitting. Ask for a tour from someone while you wait for people to arrive. Keep your energy up by moving around occasionally. It will help wake you back up for the next interview.

What I'm about to say may seem ridiculous, but this is the level of detail I consider when interviewing. When you walk into a conference room, look at the arrangement of chairs at the table. My preference is not to sit across from people during interviews. This configuration is a bit too adversarial for me. If you're at a round table, this will be less of an issue. To avoid sitting directly across from someone I'll sit at a corner of a desk, leaving the head of the table open for them. I don't sit at the head of the table, as that is traditionally a position of power and attention. I don't want that during the interview. I sit at a corner, so they have two choices where to sit: Across or on a corner. If they take the seat across from me, I can adjust positions if I desire to maintain this configuration. If they sit at the head of the table, I have the setup that I want.

This configuration is much more relaxed in terms of body language. We aren't sitting opposing one another. We point in the same direction. I want whoever I'm interviewing with to be as comfortable as possible and to reduce any amount of potential competition or conflict. By sitting at a corner with them, we can be slightly turned away from one another to provide space while also being closer to one another than if we had been across the table or desk. You'll be able to see what they're looking at on your resume and point to it. Your interview will feel more like a joint effort instead of a test.

The advice to bring a notepad and pen so you look prepared applies here as well. Place your notebook and pen on the table. It shows you are ready to get to the interview and you will be ready to take notes. What kinds of notes would you take? Jot down anything that sounds interesting about the company or job. Usually, you'll interview with multiple people in one day, so if you hear someone say something interesting, you can ask someone else. Also, you can use it to form up some more specific questions when the dreaded, "So, any questions for me," comes at the end.

Guidelines for Successful Interviews

When it comes to interviews, I may have tipped my hand a little to show how I shift the odds in my favor. I want to spend a short time outlining a few guidelines I follow that lead to successful interviews.

Since these are only guidelines, you will have to interpret them in the moment. They aren't hard and fast rules you must follow but will help you steer through emerging moments.

Here is my list of interviewing guidelines:

- Silence is death
- The more they talk, the better
- Stories over facts
- Correct is good, but likable is better
- Say what you can do, never what you cannot

Silence is Death

My first guideline is simple enough. Silence means death for you in an interview.

For many stages of the interview, the steps will be primarily focused on questions and answers, so this will come naturally. There will be times, however, when you are asked a question, and you may become tempted to think through the answer at the risk of saying something wrong. This inclination is backward. I would recommend that you begin to speak whatever is in your head as you work the problem.

Verbalization is a powerful strategy that will be your secret weapon if you have to whiteboard. When you're quiet, no information or data is flowing to the interviewer. Remember, these interviewers weren't trained or taught to interview. Imagine yourself interviewing someone. In a year you very well might be if this is your first job.

Your silence allows them to wonder what you're thinking. It leaves room for them to invent a story about your silence. Maybe they think you can't remember. Maybe they think you don't know. Maybe you're wasting their time. After all, they know the answer to the question, why is it so hard? You don't want these thoughts in their head, so talk.

Talking, even if it is the exposition of your thought process, keeps them engaged with you. Hearing you talk quiets the voices in their head as they listen to you solve the problem. Your speech acts as an invitation for them to speak. Untrained interviewers often can't resist offering advice and hints to the person solving a problem.

Talking lets them peek into how you solve problems. Even if you can't arrive at the exact solution, you'll likely say more right than wrong while you think through your answer. By saying it, the interviewer can arrive at the same conclusion.

Contrast this with dead silence until you declare an incomplete or wrong answer. In this case, the interviewer has no alternative except to assume that you didn't know the answer or that you don't know how to solve problems.

Keep talking. Silence is your death.

The More They Talk, the Better

An interesting corollary to the above guideline is that the more they talk, the better. Silence during an interview spells disaster, but if you can keep them talking, you're likely to succeed even more than if you're talking.

The untrained interviewer is prey to the same desire to be in the spotlight as everyone else. They want to enjoy the moment. Get them talking.

Here's an example dialog to show what can happen.

"Hi, I'm Andy, welcome to our little company. Can I get you anything before we begin?"

"It is great to meet you, Andy. Some water would be great, but before we begin I was wondering if I can ask a quick question?"

"Sure."

"Do you keep up with Game of Thrones? Did you see the newest episode?"

"Oh yeah! I can't believe..."

From that moment on the interviewer has engaged the interviewee in a topic they both enjoy during an interview. The time they have to assess the candidate runs low, but the interviewer is having a good time in that discussion. A well-placed question can turn an hour-long interview into an hour-long monolog by your interviewer on a topic they're passionate about.

I was interviewing at a job once with two interviewers. This particular interview was one of a series of interviews I had on the same day. After introductions and a question, I threw one question back at the two of them. They spent the remainder of my interview in dialog between themselves. I would occasionally interject a few affirmations but otherwise, I let them talk and discuss. Feedback was that they loved me and couldn't wait to bring me on.

While my example demonstrates pulling the interviewer into a discussion unrelated to work, you can draw your interviewer into a pleasant career-oriented discussion that has nothing to do with assessments of your skill. You'll speak with them as equals. This situation is in your favor, as leaving the interviewer longing to continue the conversation leaves a positive impression. When they give their input whether they'd like to work with you, they will say they do.

Whether it be unrelated to work, or a question born of curiosity about the job, find ways to draw your interviewer into conversation. As intimidating as it may be in the moment, let your curiosity take over periodically. Getting your interviewer talking is excellent for your anxiety and stress as well as increasing your chances of getting the job.

Stories Over Facts

If it isn't evident by now, a dialog is a crucial element to successful interviewing. When answering questions and engaging with your interviewers, prefer stories over facts.

Maybe you've experienced a moment when someone did something that made you angry, the kind of anger that lingers and makes you wonder, "What is wrong with them?" In that state of mind, your brain comes up with a reason for its current problem of being angry. It will construct a fictional world to justify this anger. That story is enough for your brain to feed its sense of outrage. The brain's ability to fill in gaps with stories of its choosing is what helps us process our encounters, regardless of the emotions involved.

We want to avoid letting the interviewer fill in their own gaps. By telling your story, the interviewer's mind will hook on to the details you give and use those to make sense of what they are hearing. Speaking your stories allows you to give what would otherwise be a flawed short answer, and yet it will seem reasonable and pragmatic when backed by the story. Every developer spends a significant part of their career doing things they know aren't as good as they can be. Telling an account allows you to share that same truth with them and engage them in the struggle of doing your best in a messy situation.

Your Storybook

Throughout this process I've recommended that you practice telling stories and prepared answers for the interview, but I haven't spent a lot of time going into detail about how to collect those stories.

From now on, when you're at work, keep a notebook handy and anything good that you do, no matter how small, record it with the date it happened. This is a discipline that serves many purposes. Some of those are:

- Giving you an edge in your interviews
- Negotiating higher pay
- Asking for a raise or promotion
- Building your resume
- Strengthening cover letters, portfolios, etc.

Even if it seems trivial to write down small victories, it is a practice worth developing. Really fascinating stories will emerge as you devote time to recording the good things that happen.

If you'd like, take some time and think back from this moment and start recording the good things you have contributed to. Again, don't qualify them as not good enough or too small. Just inventory them. Collect a handful that could become good stories. Practice them. Update any application materials if you need to.

Start recording those good things now!

This fundamental principle of stories over facts also has a significant impact on another principle of telling people what you can do instead of what you can't. By weaving a narrative around your strengths and history, you can show that even if you don't have what you need today, you can find it. If you stick to short answers, you'll be limited to saying that you cannot do something.

For the case where you're asked a question about something that seems factual and straightforward, you may be tempted to give a brief factual answer. I would generally regard this as a mistake unless you have extreme confidence that you're correct. The reason I suggest to avoid short factual answers is that few things in our industry are so straightforward. Many people in our industry get tripped up over nuances in word choices or want to use an exception as justification that the answer is wrong. A short answer allows you to fall victim to these behaviors in your interview.

I was interviewing for a job once, and I quickly formed the opinion that I wasn't going to work for the company. They asked a technical question, and I responded with a short answer. They didn't accept the answer, but gave me another chance to explain in more detail so they could assess my response. It turned out that my interviewer was unaware of the data structure I had named and considered my answer incorrect. After I explained how I'd build that same data structure by hand, he enjoyed the answer. I then told him that was the data structure I had named.

If I had started with a story, even if it were about the simple one-word answer, they would have followed along with me the entirety of the interview. Instead, I turned the interview into a pointed moment where I highlighted my interviewer didn't know the answers to his own questions.

Even if that case is extreme, this idea crops up in numerous places. When answering questions about your resume and other materials, respond with a story. I hope this part is obvious, but if you give short answers, you leave the rest of the story to whatever the interviewer creates in their head.

Reflect on the questions you're asked about your resume and past. Find stories to tell for those and practice them. When answering technical questions, even if you know the answer to what they're asking, answer it in the form of a story. Telling that story lets them know more about who you are and how you work. Even if the answer isn't perfect, it will show how you work through things to do the best you can.

Correct is Good, Likable is Better

Imagine having to interview someone who has all the right answers. Every single question you ask, they give you a perfect answer. It is almost scary how correct they are. Then, at the end, when you meet with people you're asked, "Do you want to work with them?" For the enlightened jerk, this is their downfall. For the likable developer, this is their boon.

Correct is good, but likable is better.

People are going to choose people they want to work with, and no amount of smarts, cleverness, or correctness is going to counter that fact. Software development happens with teams, and it happens through people solving problems together. Nobody wants to come to work only to suffer a jerk for forty hours a week.

There is another aspect of this that I want to bring up as well. A funny thing happens when you hear something good about someone. You begin to associate that same goodness to other aspects of their life. Maybe you see someone that looks perfect. Everything about their presentation is infuriatingly right. Many people will be tempted to believe, based solely on that single impression, that they must have other aspects of their life similarly put together. Their career must be great. They probably drive a great car. The list goes on. This is the halo effect.

It is how many of our brains work, so if someone likes you, they'll also believe other areas of your life are going better than they are. It is how this strange bias works.

In interviews, it's a tool in your toolbox.

If you think I'm about to cross a line where I'm basically telling you to take advantage of biases that almost everyone has so that you are more successful in an interview, I am. If you think that is wrong or unethical, I have only one thing to offer.

Interviews exist to weed you out of the process. They exist to protect the company from a bad hire. They are poorly constructed and executed by untrained people. The deck is stacked against you, even if you know how to do the job.

Beat the process, get the job, and fix the process.

If that means telling stories and being someone that charms everyone during this process, then do it. They'll happily believe that if you're that great in an interview, you must be excellent in other areas. They'll want to work with you. They'll want to hire you, and at that point, you'll have to give them an excuse to refuse you.

Likability isn't anything magical in the end. It just takes being a person who is willing to be near another person. Talk with them, listen to them, and share your stories. It's all right to laugh in interviews! Make a joke. The bar you're aiming for is to be yourself wholly in the interview. Draw them in with your sincerity. It can be scary to be yourself in an interview, but if you force your way to seem professional, it winds up being pretty obvious to the interviewer.

At this point in my career, I bring a somewhat disarming level of honesty in my interviews. In an interview, I said that a part of who I am at the job is honest. I noted that this trait means that I'll sometimes say things that other people won't, but I'll do it kindly. During one interview, I was asked how I'd drive teams to meet commitments. I said that I would neither drive teams or force commitments.

I got that job.

One of the things he said was that he appreciated how I pushed back honestly and respectfully when I thought I needed to. He didn't want someone to go along with what he said, and he wanted experts. Experts will have better answers than him, and he wants to hear them.

I could have given him the answer he wanted. Instead, I gave him, through my answer, insight into who I am, and he liked that.

Interviewers tend to overlook likability, but without it, no extent of right answers will save you.

Say What You Can Do, Never What You Cannot

At some point during the interviewing process, you'll get asked a question that you'll have no idea how to answer. It might be the pressure to answer on the spot that causes your mind to go blank. What do you do when that moment comes?

I advocate interviewing all the time as you apply for three jobs a week. That means you will be in the position to answer questions that you haven't a clue how to respond to. This situation, although unpleasant, is an opportunity for practice.

The principle here is to say what you can do and never what you cannot. When someone asks you a question that you honestly don't have the answer to, "I don't know" is both honest and terminal to a conversation. If the interviewer asked that question expecting an answer, they'll leave without one and wondering what else you don't know. We want to avoid this situation.

Not having an answer will most likely come up through technical questions. They may ask you a nuanced question about a subtle language or technology feature that honestly nobody should know. They may ask you something using words with which you're unfamiliar. They may ask you something you've never encountered. This will happen on the job, too. You'll have to solve problems you've never seen and sometimes with technology you've never used.

Think through how you'd go about solving that problem you've never seen. If this isn't your first job, then you'll likely have memories fresh in your mind. How did you go about solving a problem you had no idea how to solve? How did you learn utterly new technology?

Answering these questions gets you close to describing how you can go about answering questions or solving the problems you'll face in an interview. Where "I don't know" is terminal in a conversation, describing your approach to finding answers and solving problems opens the conversation back up. Even without the de facto solution, the interviewer can leave with the impression that you'd figure it out quickly enough. Also, they will think your resourcefulness makes up for not knowing some particular thing.

Here's an example dialog to illustrate the point:

Interviewer: Tell me about the steps of a TCP handshake.

Candidate: I'm not very familiar with the handshake process, but if I needed to find out how to solve that problem, I'd probably start by looking on Stack Overflow and Wikipedia. Stack overflow would give me a practical answer, but Wikipedia would likely give me a complete explanation. I'd hopefully be able to use the information there to make progress.

The response that the interviewer gives after this open exchange can vary wildly. The interviewer may accept the answer coldly, or they may press further on the issue trying to extract an "I don't know." They may break from the question and tell a story about how they had to deal with the same thing. I can't predict what will ever happen in a technical interview, but in the example I provided, the candidate gave insight into how they'd go about solving a new problem, which is the nature of the job.

The candidate could strengthen their response further by tying their approach back to a story in their past where they used that approach successfully. They could also highlight how not having the answers is a significant part of the job and what they bring is a high level of adaptability and an eagerness to learn from everyone around them. Expressing these sentiments can show that you have more value beyond knowing the nature of a TCP handshake.

Applying the same idea of saying what you can do to solve a problem even when you're not sure where to start combines very well with the other principles I've outlined so far when you have to whiteboard a question in front of people. By talking through what you can do to solve or try to solve the problem gives insight into your thought process. That same insight will help the interviewer stay connected with you as you find your way, and if the time runs out without a solution, there is a good chance the interviewer will leave thinking that you needed a little more time instead of assuming you had no idea.

A way to prepare for this is to look up interviewing questions that you have no idea how to answer. Then, talk through how you might go about finding the answer. Speak to what relatable knowledge or experience you can apply. Talk through the process you use to solve problems. Get comfortable talking through questions you cannot directly answer. It is only a matter of time before your future job depends on this ability.

9 - The Interview Stages

Now that I've covered the elements of successful interviewing let's look at the individual stages of the interview where you will apply the guidance. You'll experience wide variation in what I'm about to describe, but the elements will likely remain the same. In other words, many of the stages I'll describe will occur, but their order and contents will vary.

The core elements of an interviewing process go like this:

- Proof of Life
- Phone Screen
- Technical Interviews
- HR Interview
- Leadership Interview

Proof of Life

Often when a company decides to interview you, the process begins with what I call a "Proof-of-Life" interview. Someone will call you up, most likely from HR, and express their interest in interviewing you.

Past that, they may ask a few relatively simple questions about things like where you live, what you're currently doing. While many of these questions seem causal, they matter.

For example, if you apply for a job in another location and they ask where you live, by saying you live somewhere else, you may have disqualified yourself.

Many companies are only interested in local candidates. Even if you were ready, willing, and prepared to move for other reasons, they'd disqualify you. So, when they ask where you live, consider saying something like, "I currently live in so-and-so, but I was thinking about moving to the job area anyway." This statement sounds like happy circumstances are bringing you both together.

When companies ask what you're currently doing, this is your first chance to tell them how what you're doing makes you a perfect fit. This approach goes along with a broader strategy that I'll describe soon about having a story ready.

When they ask you questions, you want to be able to relate your answer back, unerringly, to the simple fact that your entire life has led you to them.

If I were applying for a job that was about Java development, but my current job had me doing more operations and system administration I might say, "Well, I've been doing Java development for years, so I decided to expand my skills a bit so I can maintain the environments my software runs in. I'm learning a lot about system administration and operations."

That statement works if, through my research, I have the impression they're interested in full-stack people, interested in DevOps, or a few other values around learning, empowerment, or growth. I can connect what I'm doing that may seem unrelated back to the job posting in a way that shows that I have even more to offer than they first thought. That is the game.

These first questions, often asked by HR, may seem conversational, yet they also provide an opportunity to increase your chances.

Even if what I just described above seems a bit overwhelming, don't worry—this first call exists to confirm that you want to interview, that you are who you said you are, and your availability for the next round of interviews.

The "Proof of life" is the easiest part of the interviewing process.

From here, things get more complicated.

The Phone Screen

After you've had a conversation with someone in HR and scheduled your interviews, you are likely to have one or more phone screens. When I say phone screen, I mean a technical phone screen. Generally, phone screens are the first real interview in the process.

While the specific contents of phone screens vary wildly, you can expect to be asked a few technical questions. Sometimes these questions will be problems you'll have to talk through, and other times they'll quiz you on knowledge or trivia. Around these technical pieces, you'll get to tell your story and ask questions at the end.

There are several categories of knowledge that I recommend almost everyone interviewing has a grasp of. The scope of knowledge you may get asked about is beyond this book, but here is a list of things I recommend looking into.

General Knowledge:

- Source control usage
- Data structures
- Sorting and searching algorithms
- Details of the language and frameworks

While your specific job will indicate more specialized knowledge, these core elements will exist in almost every technical question. Practically all coding challenges are based on your understanding of data structures and algorithms.

I want to break things down a little bit also for the broad job types. This list won't necessarily include specific technologies, but your job requirements will.

Back-end:

- Cacheing
- Design patterns
- Performance optimizations
- Database design
- Services and Microservices
- API design and testing
- XML and JSON usage
- Error handling and exceptions

Front-end:

- MVC, MVVM, and other patterns
- Package management
- CSS, Less, Sass
- Semantic HTML
- Usability and design
- JavaScript knowledge

DevOps/Full-Stack:

- Cloud services
- Configuration management
- Automation and pipelines
- Networking and firewalls
- Failover
- Blue-Green and rolling deployments
- Monitoring and alerts

These topics are fairly general, but I think they cover some of the most likely candidate topics.

The Front-End Challenge

I want to take a brief moment to talk about Front-end development. This particular career path comes with some specific challenges in the industry which are worth noting. The reason I bring this up is that Front-end blends several disciplines at once. On the one hand, front-end developers are writing source code like anyone else. They also may be doing the visual design. This broad spectrum of activities can lead to confusing interviews.

There are two basic categories that front-end development interviews tend to fall into. First, and most commonly, interviewers will treat you as though you are purely a developer. By this I mean the questions will be focused exclusively on programming, JavaScript, and how a specific technology works. The second category is when interviewers interview you as though you are a designer. They may ask a few coding questions, but most are going to focus on how you go about making things look pixel-perfect and your expertise with things like CSS.

For the unaware front-end developer, they may get caught off-guard by these questions. I attribute this divergence in interviews with the relative newness of front-end development as a separate field. Many companies are still making sense of what front-end means to them. The people who interview you will interview you based on their strengths more than the needs of the job.

After some introductory remarks during your phone screen, you'll be asked your first question. I recommend that before saying a single word, even if you're confident of the answer, that you take a breath. Don't hurry through any of this. You want as much time to think through your response and what you'll say. Taking one breath gives you that. It also will help you relax if the pressure has built up.

From here, as in all of the interviewing process, you're trying to get a yes. So answer the questions using the guidelines and techniques I've listed. By applying them, you can have an unclear answer to a question they ask and still give the impression that you're the right fit for the job and move to the next stage. That is the goal in this phone screen, to progress to the next interview.

While interviewing, have paper and a pen nearby. Write notes about the technical questions you're asked. This practice will build a study guide for you. Having a study guide serves two primary purposes. Recording the questions helps you prepare for future interviews as you can then study for the question and develop an answer that you're comfortable saying. Second, by learning the answers to these questions, you're exposing yourself to new areas of software development that you may not have known about or had a chance to study.

I remember when I was first starting, there was a question that would flummox me every time I heard it. The question was, "What is the difference between an abstract class and an interface?" I knew the answer, but every time I heard it, my head would flood with doubt. I'd wonder if I knew the answer, or there was something that I'd missed in the question that would embarrass me later. I heard this same question in several interviews. Eventually, I sat down with it, practiced my answer, developed a more intuitive understanding of that answer, and never made a mistake with it again.

When it comes to the phone screen, record the questions so you can practice, focus on the guidelines and advice I've outlined, and treat the experience as practice. Success here is progressing to the next interview. You don't have to have all the answers, but you do have to convince them that you're worth learning more about.

Technical Interviews

After a phone screen, you are likely to have a series of in-person interviews all within one day. You may also have these over video calls. These interviews will be conducted by several people to assess your technical abilities and to see if you're someone they want to work with. These interviews are what I'm calling, "Technical Interviews."

Expect in these interviews to talk through your resume. Have stories ready to highlight your strengths for each job you have. Be prepared to answer questions about specifics within your resume as well. If you've put numbers down to show some impact, anticipate that they'll ask you how you arrived at those numbers. All the advice I gave in previous chapters about using your resume, cover letter, and secondary material to stage questions will bear fruit at this moment.

You'll find that you continually get asked about a few particular points from your application packet, and other elements are ignored. You can use this information to strengthen your entire application package.

Beyond that, you'll be asked a series of technical questions. Some of these questions will be like the ones described in the phone interview section, but you'll be answering them face-to-face. The pressure and stress tend to get a little higher when you're answering in person. Also, during these interviews, the questions will tend to move beyond factual questions and veer more into the realm of having you talk through solving or how you solve a problem.

Expect questions to come from the same topics I listed in phone interviews, but start with a phrase similar to, "How have you..." or, "How would you...?" One example that comes up quite often in interviews is, "How have you used branches in Git?"

These questions are blurring the lines of knowing facts and their application. This moment is where your effort in building stories can pay off.

If an interviewer asks a question you can relate to a story, tell that story.

Another common question you might bump into goes something like, "How would you remove all the duplicate items from a list/array?" This question again blurs the lines a little bit. There is a straightforward answer, but also an opportunity to talk through how you arrived at your answer. Talking through your reasons and the process you've used is just as important as the answer itself.

You'll have to speak through your resume and other application package materials, field some technical questions that begin to speak more to how you work, and then come the big moments— whiteboarding and pairing.

Whiteboarding

This activity is probably the most dreaded of all technical interviewing practices. It is terrible for the candidate and gives terrible information to the interviewer. The basic premise is that you'll have to solve a programming problem by writing the code on a whiteboard. You won't have a computer or access to any information. You'll solve it by hand while you're watched, and you have a finite amount of time.

Thankfully this is a skill you can practice. I would love for everyone with this book never to struggle with whiteboarding again so that the practice falls out of use.

First, you can practice this at home. While you won't get the same sense of pressure and stress, you can still get comfortable with the awkwardness of solving a problem by hand in front of someone. If you want to practice at home, look up simple programming problems, set a timer for thirty minutes, and start solving it with a pen and paper. If you want to up the ante a bit, do this same activity while someone is watching you. Permit them to interrupt you with a question now and then. The questions don't matter, because you're learning how to accommodate an interruption and get back to work.

There are a few bits of advice I want to emphasize here, even if they're written about in more detail in other places. Whiteboarding is so stressful it deserves repetition. When I mentor people in whiteboarding interviews, I give them a few specific pieces of advice.

- Keep talking
- Know your data structures
- Never write real code

I've given the advice to keep talking many times before, and it is critical during whiteboarding. *I want you to say out loud every thought you have when it comes to solving this problem.* You may generally be a quiet person, but when you have to whiteboard, talk. The reason I insist on speaking non-stop is that it shows the interviewer what you're thinking through. A good thought process makes up for a mistaken implementation.

If you are silent through the exercise and show any signs of struggle, the interviewer will come up with their own reason for that struggle. Whatever reason they come up with will be less favorable than the story they are involved in through your constant speech.

Knowing data structures is critical to the types of questions you are likely going to encounter. Almost every technical problem you'll have to solve relies on your knowledge and application of data structures. Knowing the primary types and when to use them are cornerstones of solving almost every whiteboarding problem you'll have to answer.

If you want a list of which to learn about I'd recommend you learn them in this order:

1. Lists
2. Maps/Dictionary/Hash
3. Set
4. Linked List
5. Stacks and Queues
6. Trees
7. Graphs

I ordered this list based on my perspective of the likelihood that you'll use one of these data structures in the successful implementation of a technical problem. A linked list is a somewhat odd one for me to identify specifically, but it is a foundational data structure that tends to show up in a lot of interviews indirectly. Being comfortable with that will help you with some specific linked list questions, as well as help you solve some more interesting problems as well. The data structures I've listed after the linked list are less common in interviews as they tend to be too complicated for a problem that is solvable quickly.

My last bit of advice is that you never write code during a whiteboarding interview. If you do have to write code, write it in a language your interviewer doesn't know.

Software developers use computers to write code. They don't use a whiteboard. Your ability to write correct code on a whiteboard will never be good enough, and it shouldn't be. Don't give your interviewer an excuse to think poorly of you because you forgot a semicolon. Start writing it in "Pseudocode," and confirm if that is alright with them.

If you're unfamiliar with pseudocode, it is writing the intent of your code instead of writing actual code. A few lines of pseudocode could look something like:

```
if isRaining -> get umbrella
```

You can use whatever notation you want when writing pseudocode because it is meant to convey intent, and you're talking through it anyway. This tactic will save you time and energy through the process while removing the possibility of making a trivial mistake because you can't remember all of the syntax and libraries of a language.

If they insist, on the other hand, that you write using code, try to guess a language they don't use enough to check you on and use that one instead. The interviewer may not allow it, but it is worth a shot. Using a language they are unfamiliar with buys you the same flexibility as using pseudocode.

I was once in an interview where I had to whiteboard a problem, and the job was primarily going to be in Java. I started writing Python on the board. My interviewer said they weren't familiar with Python, and I assured them they'd pick it up. I was able to write my solution without worrying about syntax and also leveraging certain features that I knew existed within Python that my interviewer did not.

Another time as I was interviewing for a position, the interviewer asked me a database question. I've never really invested a lot of time in learning how to best use relational databases, so I said, "Well, I think I'd use a document store instead." They had never heard of that, so I showed a solution using a different type of technology. My answer surprised the interviewer as my choice of technology removed the problem entirely. At the same time, they enjoyed that I had more than one tool I could use and that I had some new knowledge to share.

So, as much as you can when whiteboarding, keep talking, have a good understanding of your data structures, and never write actual code. Practice solving problems with pen and paper to get comfortable with the awkwardness. Practice in front of someone to get used to being watched. Let them interrupt you with questions to derail you.

Whiteboarding is one of the most challenging activities within the interviewing process. While this advice will not make it painless, it will significantly improve your chances of success.

Pair Programming

For years people have been saying rightly that whiteboarding is a terrible way to conduct technical interviews, and a better way would be to sit down and work together on a problem. This slow outcry has led to an adoption of the pairing interview.

The pairing interview is when you will sit down at a computer with your interviewer and solve a problem together as though you were working together any day. First, this approach is superior to whiteboarding in that you'll be able to use a computer instead of trying to write code by hand. Second, instead of being judged from afar, you'll have someone invested in the outcome of the problem's solution. Lastly, it shows more about how you work instead of the ability to solve the problem. All of this is to your benefit.

Now, when it comes to pairing together, there are still obstacles to work through. Namely, that you'll be working on an unfamiliar configuration on a system that is new to you, and that will feel awkward and clumsy. To prepare for this possibility, do clean installs of software you're likely to encounter in the interview and acclimate yourself to that. It is also great to talk shop around what configurations, bindings, and preferences you have in software development. Aside from a few topics that seem to be irrational, like how to handle whitespace, branching, or commit messages, almost everything else is a topic of interest and discussion. Having that conversation lines up perfectly with the other principles and guidelines I've shown you already.

Also, after you've solved a problem or taken a step, ask them what shortcuts or features of their editors they would have used to accomplish the same thing. I suggest this question over, "How would you have solved it," because they can't tell you the answer to the problem, but they can show off their workflow to you. This tactic collaboratively engages them, allows them to show you some new things, they feel like they're helping you, and you are also productive. These are all great things that aid your chances of getting approval when they are asked the question, "Do you want to work with them?"

Aside from having proximity to engage your partner, the same remaining principles apply to work as a pair as they do in white-boarding. One thing I'd suggest is that when pairing, you are ideally working with your partner to solve the problem. So, while I would say keep talking while you are whiteboarding, I'd amend that to say that you should keep dialoguing with your partner when pairing. Discussing with your partner is core to pair-programming anyway, but during an interview, it is something they're likely to look for explicitly.

Another thing to consider if you're set up to pair with someone is to establish the rules you'll follow when pairing. When you're working so closely together, knowing what to expect and how best to work together can save lots of awkwardness and failures to connect. Before beginning to pair with new people, I ask, "Before we pair, can I ask what makes pairing together work well for you?" This question will prompt a look of confusion on your interviewer's face. Let the silence lie for a moment. Let them speak. Accept what they say and then say a few things about how you would prefer to work as well. End that brief conversation with, "I try to ask that question so that we can pair as effectively as possible from the beginning." This small practice will show that you're considerate, professional, and willing to do what it takes to work to the best of your ability.

Assignments

While not officially part of a technical interview, you may be asked to do an assignment in advance of the interview. You may also get asked some questions about it during your interview, though this isn't a guarantee. So, let us talk about how to do your best in a technical assignment.

The principles I've already discussed still apply, but you'll have to use them differently. Namely, your assignment won't happen in person, so keeping a dialogue going looks very different. I recommend sending periodic emails to the company about the task. When you get the assignment, you may need to immediately follow-up with an acknowledgment that you have it, and ask for someone you can send some clarifying questions to. From there, you can occasionally send updates or inquiries. I think, during an assignment, there is a line between communicating enough to show that you're engaged while thinking through the problem and bothering them. For any given assignment I've personally had, I think I've sent roughly three emails to them. One was that initial receipt and request for contact. Another was to ask some clarifying questions, and the third was a fairly comprehensive email that went into detail about my submission.

What I'd caution against is sending no communication at all. The reasoning is that the requirements you receive may either be very confusing, or worse, just clear enough that you think you understand them. If you send no email to clarify, then you may submit a completely wrong assignment. I've received a clarification that thoroughly changed my direction enough times now that I send that email. The same is true of the people I've mentored. Also, if you send your submission in and they read your code, they may form an opinion about your competence based solely on the code you wrote. That opinion will be something you have no say in developing. If you engage them even slightly in communication, your communication will also influence their opinion. For example, say they see your code and think that some piece is terrible. Your interviewer may then believe that your coding abilities are not adequate. However, if you send some communication that shows that you've thought through the problem, then they will also likely realize that this bit of terrible code is just a small mistake you can correct.

If you're silent, you have no say in the opinion they form of you.

One last bit of tactical advice when it comes to communication about assignments is regarding timelines. Often the first communication I send out is that receipt that I have the assignment. I also ask clarifying questions, and I also give some indication as to my schedule. I make it a point to highlight that I have other commitments in my life. I aim to remove any expectation that I've dropped everything, and that I'm working on their assignment from that point forward. So if I receive an assignment that they say should take three hours, I send an email saying that I'll work on it in between my other commitments. I have work, a family, friends, and other obligations. I don't stop my life because I have an assignment, and neither should you. I set the expectation outright that I'll work in between my commitments in that first communication to prevent them from wondering what I'm doing and where my assignment is.

Beyond maintaining clear communication throughout the assignment, I want to highlight a few key elements of success to add to your assignment:

- Solve first, fix second
- Smallest possible problems
- Ignore the timeline
- Document for a stranger
- Write a readme
- GitHub is public
- Automated tests are gold

Solve First, Fix Second

One of the main things I see people struggle with when trying to complete an assignment is that they get trapped trying to write good code instead of focusing on writing working code. A poorly written but functional assignment is better than well-written code that doesn't solve the problem.

When working through an assignment, and on the job, I advocate that you focus on getting to any workable solution before trying to clean it up. Don't worry about how bad you think your code is, or how many rules you think you're breaking, focus on solving the problem first. Once you have a working solution, then fix it.

One of the problems that comes with trying to fix as you go is that unless you're very thoughtful about your approach, you'll introduce bugs into your code as you work. You may start by writing a line of code you're not proud of, and in the act of cleaning it up, introduce a problem. How would you know if this happened?

A way to prevent that is to get a solution built first, and then re-verify as you clean up. Now, your solution remains valid as you clean up bits of code, refactor, and you can even try an alternative that you think is better. Having a working baseline is like a safety net. Also if you feel like you don't have time, you at least have something working.

Smallest Problems First

Another critical strategy for working through an assignment is to solve the smallest possible problems first. There is a tendency in many software developers to try to solve problems that take days to solve by themselves. Imagine, for the sake of this section, that writing software is like placing a bet.

If you take on a massive problem, you are similarly placing a large bet. Your currency is time. If your bet was that you'd have solved this particular problem in two days, and you lose that bet, you've also lost two days. You can't get those back. You can't rewind the clock on that. You have to start over again with what you've learned. You have to place a new bet.

Consider then, placing a bet for the next hour of your time and solving a problem that only takes an hour. It may not be all aspects of a problem, but some portion of it. Some piece that you can verify. If you lose that bet, you've only lost an hour and can recover very quickly. This approach is the winning strategy here.

Many coding assignments will have you do networking calls with external systems. Developers often treat this networking as one whole problem to solve. This decision is a big bet. By mentally committing oneself to this immense problem, all progress is going to measured by one's ability to complete that one entire problem in one attempt. It is unlikely to go well.

Take that same idea of networking with another system, and instead break it down into smaller bets. Here is a potential list of more minor problems that you could attempt that in total, solve the entire thing:

- Authentication
- Getting any data back with any mechanism
- Getting any data back through code
- Getting the right data back through code
- Adding query parameters for more specific data

There are potentially more depending on how involved the problem is, but each of those smaller problems is a lot more approachable than one singularly large API problem.

I'll also highlight that one of these steps was to get things to work with any mechanism. When you're solving problems, you want to solve for as few variables at a time as possible. That simplifies your effort. When I say to get data back by any mechanism, I'm specifically recommending that you get data back without writing code. Use a browser or a tool like cURL to get your data back the first time. That confirms you understand the API without adding the variable of correct code. Now, when you do write it in code, you know what should happen. This approach gives way more confidence than trying to do both at the same time.

Admittedly learning to break a problem down takes time, but one way I describe it is to break the problem down until it seems boring and like a chore to solve. As unappealing as that is, it also means you've broken it down to a level that is trivial and comfortable to you based on your knowledge and experience. The more familiar the problem is, the less you'll need to break it down. The more difficult it sounds, the more you'll find yourself breaking it down.

Ignore the Timeline

Most homework assignments come with a deadline attached. Sometimes they are framed with a precise due date, and other times they are given with an implied due date. An explicit one would look something like, "Have your assignment turned into us by 5:00 pm on April 10th." An implicit one will look like, "Take as long as you need, but don't spend more than three hours on it."

Ignore both.

There may be consequences to missing the date, but if you find yourself stressed out because of the date, you may make more mistakes than you would otherwise. You may also find yourself cutting corners to meet the deadline. I'd rather you not stress out and make mistakes. After all, this interview will be one of many.

So, will there be consequences if you miss the date? Yes, probably. The reality is that I've known people who still interviewed with companies even after they submitted late, and I've met others who never heard back. I can't predict how companies will handle this scenario, so all you can do is manage yourself.

Assignments with firm deadlines likely need to be taken a bit more seriously, but the implied deadlines are outright ignorable. Just because they say it takes three hours or whatever has no bearing on reality, and they will almost never tell you to prove how long it took. This possibility may come as a shock to you, but when they chose that problem, they most likely didn't time themselves solving it.

With all that in mind, you know how you work best, so if the deadline and pressure that comes with it is a healthy motivator, then use it. If it adds an unproductive amount of stress and anxiety, try to ignore the deadline entirely. There are plenty of cases out there where a late submission didn't hold the candidate back.

Document for Strangers

When on the job, you'll often see code and think, "What idiot wrote this?" You may find out that you were that idiot just three months ago. Reading code invites strong reactions in the reader. Documenting your assignment helps put context in place so that your readers don't have that same kind of response.

I recommend that you document anything confusing or hard for you to write. If you wrote a method that took time to figure out and had tricky parts to get right, it needs documentation. It probably also needs to be cleaned up and refactored, but that's in an earlier section. So put some comments above your method explaining what the intent of your code is, and why it is tricky.

Document variables that aren't completely obvious through their name and usage. You'll likely find that twenty percent or more of your variables fall into that category. Add a line comment where you declare your variable that says its intended use.

You may have noticed that I've used the word intent several times for documentation. That is because when someone reads your code, they'll want to know what that code does and why you wrote it that way. The first of those questions is intent. What is the point of that code? What do you want to do? The second part about why you wrote it often doesn't deserve a lot of documentation if you write about the intent. The intent gives enough context to justify the detailed choices most of the time.

The last thing I recommend you document is any errors or exception cases. The reasoning is that it shows you've given thought into how your code operates in less than ideal circumstances, and how someone might handle that scenario if they used your code. It shows a level of forethought and experience that is uncommon in many submissions.

Many people who write code comment out a lot of the code they don't want as they work. They like to keep the old code around as a reference. Also, they may add to-do comments or things like that. Before you submit your code, remove all of that. Don't submit anything with commented code, to-dos, or little notes to yourself. These things will be regarded as unprofessional by your readers. Ironically, the same people who may judge you will work that way on the job. The difference is that many times on the job, developers strip out those things before releasing code, and submitting your assignment is a release.

Write a Readme

Related to documentation is writing a readme. You'll make thousands of decisions when building your solution to the assignment, and without a little extra help and information, your readers may form a poor opinion of you. Writing a readme helps with that.

The elements of a good readme include:

- A guide to run your software
- Notes about the overall design of your code
- A bit about the tradeoffs you made

- Where you'd go next

These four elements provide essential information that your reader will need to judge your assignment fairly.

When writing about how to run the software, I want you to write it as though you weren't writing for an expert. Write it as though someone less experienced than yourself was attempting to execute your project for the first time. List any dependencies they need and where to get them. List any instructions they have to type and configurations they have to enter. You are trying to make this as brainless as possible. This approach isn't insulting to anyone and is quite the opposite. If you can provide documentation to me that is so easy to follow that I don't have to work hard, that goes a long way in my book.

Then comes writing about the design of your code. For me, the main things to pay attention to here are to describe your approach to the problem in a few words, and how the main files or classes accomplish their goals. You don't have to get into gory details about which functions and classes work with what, but you can say that your RestService class is responsible for interacting with APIs, and that's good enough. This removes any guesswork for your reader as they look at your code. When you write the intent in your documentation, your reviewer can look past imperfection and understand the purpose behind the code.

Next come the tradeoffs and where to go next. These last bits are where you can leave a more personal note for the interviewers as to what was going on as you wrote your solution. This extra documentation gives them insight into how you work and the choices you made to complete the assignment.

There isn't any particular magic to this section. I tend to write about anything I decided to stop putting more time into, or that I'd come back to, or that I wasn't going to come back to and clean up. If I cut corners, this is where I'd list that. For the RestService example that

I listed above, I might put in this section that while the RestService works for this example, I should have made it more generic and that if a new request came in for more APIs, I'd probably make it an interface.

That little bit is all it takes to give background to the choices I made, and it also shows that I'm thinking ahead about how to improve the code. Including where you'd spend time next is valuable as well. It is one thing to explain how you came to the condition your code is in, and another to show that you've already started thinking about where to go next. It shows that you're aware of your choices and trade-offs as well as the remedies to them. These are all signs that you have more experience and maturity beyond the code that you've submitted.

GitHub is Public

Sometimes you'll be asked to submit your code through a public service like GitHub. While this fine, it does invite a question. If yours is public on GitHub, isn't everyone else's?

The answer is, yes, they are.

Everyone has to weigh the potential for unethical behavior here, but if you've been asked to submit your code through a public forum like GitHub, you can very easily search for others' code too.

If you use someone else's code that isn't explicitly licensed as open-source, you're cheating and potentially violating copyright. If your future employer thinks along my lines and finds out, you're finished. Also, people within that company will talk about it. If you bump into those people again, they'll remember you as the person who tried to steal someone else's work to get the job.

Now, I do think that if the information is publicly available, you can read it. I have no problem reading someone else's code for how they got through a problem and then implementing my solution.

If you've ever used Google or StackOverflow, you've done exactly this, and it is a normal thing to do.

I've never confronted a company about this particular prospect to know their take on it. I don't believe they think it through when they request you to put your code on a publicly searchable system.

As a small aside, I do know someone who would take other people's work from GitHub and pass it off as their own to attempt to get hired. I suspect the kind of person who does this has other issues too, but I never really heard of them getting a job, or if they got caught. Don't be this person.

Automated Testing is Gold

At the end of the day, you'll have to submit your assignment in some condition. Even if you followed all of my advice diligently, you might wonder if it was good enough or if there was something more you could do. This is where automated testing comes in. Automated testing separates your assignment from others by a large margin.

When you submit your code without automated tests, you're leaving the reader to assume you did some testing by hand before you submitted it. If they then find an obvious problem, they'll wonder if you tested it at all. This realization isn't a good train of thought for your interviewer to explore when it concerns your future employment. If, however, you've provided automated tests, you have executable proof that you've tested your software.

Now, in your education so far in software development, I assume you've bumped into automated testing at some point. If not, I recommend learning about automated unit testing and, even more specifically, test-driven-development[18]. Automated testing is nearly ubiquitous at this point in software development, so

---

[18]https://en.wikipedia.org/wiki/Test-driven_development

you might as well show that you can do it now. Test-driven-development, on the other hand, is often cited in every single job posting. It is generally regarded as a best practice but rarely seen in a job situation. In my opinion, test-driven-development will put you on an accelerated career path, while also turning assignments into a much more enjoyable experience.

If you've got your assignment ready, add some automated unit tests. Confirm they work by running them and seeing them pass. This act will show your interviewer that you've not only got the experience to solve problems, but the discipline to test them in a way that is consistent with the industry. This addition removes almost all doubt from the interviewer's mind that you have the right skills to be a good software developer.

While I can't confirm this is true, I'd personally suspect that a candidate who submitted an incomplete but thoroughly tested assignment would be near as favored as a complete but untested assignment. That is how highly I want to emphasize automated unit testing. The reason I suspect that this might be the case is that the incomplete assignment will show that you only needed more time. The complete, but untested solution may have bugs that the interviewer finds and causes a pause in the interviewer.

Often on the job, we have to create tested solutions that are hidden by configurations, feature flags, or not integrated with other code as a strategy during work. We have to be able to show that the code we're building will work when we do finally get ready to ship it and turn it on. This moment is where all of this automated testing comes in. By writing tests, you're showing you're ready to join the company today instead of being taught how to test your software.

HR Interview

After you've survived the gauntlet of technical interviews, you'll likely have one more interview with someone from human resources. This interview can be rather disarming and carries some risk when it comes to the job.

Generally speaking, the human resources interview will be about the nature of your employment. They'll want to know things about where you live, if you have to relocate, your salary requirements, and a few other things. While most of these questions are harmless, here are a few tips that will help you navigate this interview to set yourself up successfully.

In general, the same rules that I've outlined in the technical interview apply here. In particular, when you're asked pointed questions about things like salary or where you live, I want you to realize that you are speaking to someone who has a say in your employment. So, answer the questions around policy, location, and salary with what you can do and are willing to do and refrain from saying what you cannot do.

Location

The location questions deserve special attention. Often, you may apply for a job that isn't where you live. Many companies will ignore you if you aren't in the same geographic area. You'll discover this with your resume as you apply. So if you find yourself interviewing for a job that is somewhere else and you get asked where you live, a flat answer of your location will be less favorable than saying that you were thinking of moving to where they are located.

Your Salary

Salary is also a question I want to highlight. If you're interested in salary negotiation, you need to keep the discussion at a high level and without any numbers. The reason is the golden rule of negotiation: Whoever gives a number first, loses. Human resources will ask, pry, plead, and demand that you give a salary target or history. They may not always be allowed to do that, but they are trained to interview. Human Resources can be some of the hardest to evade in an interview, even if they have some of the least authority in it. If you give a number to one of these questions, it will be the number that anchors you in all future discussions. If you name a salary that you made that is higher than they make, they may disqualify you as unaffordable. If you make less, they may wonder if you're qualified. Saying your salary only ever hurts you. You have no idea what they are willing to pay for you. Only they know that, but if you say a number, they have all the information. When I'm asked about salary targets, my response is, "I'm more interested in finding out if we're a good fit for one another. If we decide we want to work together, we'll find a number that works."

You may find that in the moment, it is difficult to hold firm to an answer like that. In that case, I recommend having a number in your head that is your absolute minimum target, and then add something on top of that. If they go below your minimum, you walk away knowing that it wasn't worth it. You add an amount on top of that because living on the minimum will always make you wonder if you should have had more.

All this advice around salary applies when you want to negotiate salary. I don't necessarily recommend you do so on your first job, as it is very stressful, and you could lose that first job over it. If you're interested, setting yourself up successfully now by not giving a number is crucial.

Personality and Fit

Beyond location and salary, you might be asked some personality questions that, with a little practice and a few stories, you'll navigate with ease. Two such questions that are almost always going to come up are:

- What challenging situation have you encountered at work, and how did you handle it?
- Where do you see yourself in two years?

For the first question, you'll likely find plenty of previous life experiences that you'd describe as challenging. What I want you to do is think about the story you tell where it ends with you being better for the experience. By all means, show your mistakes, talk about how it was hard, but get to the part where you found your way through it. Highlight what you learned, your strengths, and the awareness you developed from that experience.

The second question stumped me for a long time in my career. I honestly had a hard time coming up with anything more than "Employed." I had to think long and hard about what my career goals really were. I then worked backward from an ideal career to two years away. Try that. Then you can speak to who you want to become. This question, though, has something subtle behind it as well. Someone in human resources is asking you where you see yourself in the near horizon. Think they want to hear the answer, "At another company getting paid more for the same job"? No, they do not. So, even if you think your goals take you to other places, find a version of it going with this company most of the way there.

Leadership Interview

Sometimes you'll have, after all of the other interviews, a leadership interview. This interview could be with a manager, director, vice president, or even CEO. These interviews usually end the day or process and can contain any number of components.

If this interview happens at a different point than all the others, then they want to know you before they give you the offer. You can assume you've earned all the yeses you need at this point, and you are currently introducing yourself to leadership at this interview.

On the other hand, if this interview happens alongside all the others, you may find yourself with a mixture of high-level technical questions and personality questions. It truly depends on what level of leadership they hold. The rules and guidelines I've outlined above apply here. Keep them talking, stay likable, and so on.

What is difficult about these interviews is that leaders have a lot of authority over you getting hired. So even if the interview seems simple or strangely not like an interview at all, they could leave with an impression that causes them to veto you as a candidate. Until you have the written offer, nothing is guaranteed, so stay alert even through this stage.

Asking Questions

At the end of each stage of your interview, you'll hear, "So, do you have any questions for me?" You want to have a few questions ready for this. Surprisingly, having no questions is sometimes frowned upon, so let us get a few questions prepared.

Remember when I mentioned bringing pen and paper? Well, this is one of the few good uses for it. As you interview, listen to anything interesting and make a note. At this point, ask a question about those things. Aside from that, you can also ask questions about anything you found through your research. Ask about perks they listed, or the direction of the company, or when they adopted some relatively new technology. These are questions unique to them that you can bring.

Aside from that, there are a few canned questions you can always have at the ready. Some of the ones that I use are:

- What do you enjoy most about working here?
- If you could change anything about the company, what would it be?
- Tell me about the last late night you had here.
- What training and growth opportunities exist?
- What does the career path for my role look like?
- What does a typical day look like for you here?

These questions all exist to indirectly give me information I can use to assess what working here might be like. I highly recommend that you take some time and think about the work environment that you desire. Then, formulate some open-ended questions like the ones above that will help you figure out how this future job compares to that ideal. You may find that you don't want to work here, or that even with the mess that it is good enough. At least you won't be surprised.

Throughout the interview process, you are interviewing them too. This formal time when interviewers give you the chance to ask questions is an opportunity for the savvy candidate. If you are able to execute the principles and guidelines outlined already, they will have been talking to you the entirety of the interview, and because they may be untrained, they will disclose things to you that help you find out how this company actually is.

What you'll likely find is that you'll be prompted to ask questions with just a few minutes left in the interview, so you may only be able to ask one. I always think it's somewhat amusing to make my next interviewer wait because my current one is enjoying the conversation so much.

I'll share another way to go about this that is a bit odd. Quite regularly, I don't have any real questions that would change my mind about the job. My way of handling the moment is to laugh and remark how I actually enjoy a lot of mystery in my life, so I'm content to see how the rest of this plays out. Almost without fail, this is met with, "Wow, okay. I could never do that!" The point is that this approach is consistent with my previous principles and guidelines in that I don't say what I cannot do, and I do say what I can. I say I can live with a mystery without saying I cannot ask a question.

Whether you take my strange path of saying you can live with mystery or you pull from any number of questions to ask, find ways to learn more about the company you're potentially going to work for. This last moment when they seek your questions is a failsafe for you to get clear information you can use to decide if you want to work here or not.

Summary

The technical interview is one of the most exhausting and challenging parts of getting a job. Thankfully, the plan that I outlined in *The Plan* means plenty of practice before you go for the job you desire.

Your attitude, energy, awareness, and sincerity are what allow you to succeed. I've provided guidelines, principles, and specific advice for each step of the process to help you get to the point that you can get an offer sooner. What comes next is getting the practice that can only come from interviewing.

I think it is important to reiterate a core piece of this strategy, which is that you are practicing these steps by going through actual interviews. By applying and interviewing for jobs that you're not passionate about, you can stay less invested in the outcome of getting a job or not, and stay focused at becoming an expert at navigating the process so that when you do find a job you're truly passionate about, you will get it.

Interviews can be a very tiring process, so I find it helpful to take this practicing-the-method attitude. I feel like my fatigue reminds me that I'm working on getting better and not that I may or may not have gotten the job.

For people early in their careers, few things change. Sometimes the technical questions get harder as your seniority goes up, but the process is the same. It feels the same to me even after all these years. The main change is when it comes to setting yourself up for negotiation and being more comfortable with who you are.

At this point, with interviews, I am adversarial at best. I know how the steps work well enough to use them to my benefit. I exploit the fact that the people who interview me aren't trained. I give leaders ultimatums about working with me, and I tell Human Resources that in two years, they can't afford me. I still get hired. I bring this up because what I've written is an approachable path for people early in their career to get more jobs, but it isn't the only way to go. As you get more comfortable in who you are in your career, these guidelines and principles apply less and less. The reason is that you know how valuable you are, and the industry does as well. The game changes when you realize you have more cards than your future employer.

10 - The Offer & Negotiating

All that hard work you've put in has paid off when you have an offer in hand. You earned all the yeses you needed, and now it is time to look at the offer, potentially negotiate, and sign the offer to start your job.

Before signing on the bottom line, there are some things I want to draw your attention to. Receiving the offer is the point at which you'll see more clearly what you're going to do for the company and decide if you are going to negotiate or not.

The Offer Letter

When you look at your offer letter, it will likely contain a few key elements. The items I want to draw your attention to are:

- Start date
- Compensation
- Expiration

The start date will likely be something that you've already discussed throughout your interview, but it is good to double-check that date now. Double-checking is especially true if you are relocating for the job. Generally, companies prefer to have employees start on Monday and have people's last day on Friday. If your start date is a Wednesday, you may want to check to see if that was intentional, or they would prefer it be the following Monday. Sometimes the date is selected because it falls in line with the standard two-week notice or that there is some other circumstance they are planning around. Either way, check the date and make sure there are no surprises.

The compensation is the star of the show in the offer letter. This section is where the company will describe to you your salary and other compensation like stock, equity, or bonuses. You may also see things like your paid-time-off amount here too. I don't think I've ever had an issue with any of these numbers being different than what was discussed, but it'd be terrible to find out that you are getting paid less than you thought because you didn't check in the letter.

Lastly, in some offer letters, you'll find an expiration. You'll either see this in the email that you receive with the letter or see it in the offer itself. The most common expiration period I see is forty-eight hours. That means you have forty-eight hours from the moment you receive the letter to return it, or the offer isn't valid. I want to say that I find this to be an obnoxious practice.

Choosing to work for a company is a significant decision that often includes families, budgets, and planning the exit of your existing job. The expiration, in my opinion, adds unnecessary stress. When I receive an offer with an expiration, I call up immediately and tell them the latest moment I intend to give them an answer. That may be outside of the expiration, but I make it clear they'll know one way or another from me soon. If they want to yank the offer, they can, and I'll consider myself spared from a company with poor policies.

You may also find that you get an offer on a Friday that has an expiration of forty-eight hours. I like to call the company up and ask who is working on Sunday to receive my letter. That conversation usually makes it obvious that this policy wasn't thought about before they sent it, and it is unreasonable to have a forty-eight-hour expiration. The point is, you don't have to accept the offer in terms of expiration, and you can set terms with them.

From the company's perspective, they are trying to prevent people from sitting on an offer. If you received an offer and said nothing for two weeks, the company has to figure out if they should keep interviewing even though they have a candidate they want. This limbo situation is costly for a company to be in as interviewing is expensive, but they don't know to stop since you aren't signing the offer. Throughout the hiring process, companies generally have all the information and power, which is difficult for a candidate to navigate. A company feeling uneasy here, in the end, doesn't prompt any sympathy from me.

At the bottom of the letter, you'll have a line to sign with a date. Until this letter is signed, nothing is official, and you do not have a job. So celebrate that you have the offer, but if it isn't signed, you're not finished yet.

The Benefits

I mentioned above that you'd likely see your compensation in your offer letter. Your salary is one of the main components, but it isn't the only thing that you need to look at when signing an offer. Generally, the elements that I want you to look at are:

- Salary
- Bonus
- Stock and Equity
- Vacation and Sick leave
- Health Care
- Retirement

The salary we've already covered above, the main thing is to see that it is the salary you'll accept or negotiate from as a base. You may view it written in terms of what you'll make each pay period or what you'll make per year. Either way, check the math and see that it works out and that you're comfortable with the number.

Bonus

Depending on what industry you go into and your seniority, you may find yourself looking at a bonus in your compensation package. Bonuses are rare for software development, but I'm covering it because it might pop up at some point in your career.

Bonuses are typically listed as a percentage of your income. So if you were making one-hundred thousand with a ten percent bonus, then you could be looking at an extra ten thousand dollars at some point in the year.

Now, it can get more complex than this, but for the sake of the offer letter and compensation, this level of detail is sufficient.

The way bonuses typically are paid out is a bit more interesting, and it gives clues as to how likely you'll be to receive one. When the company decides to offer a bonus, they pool the money available for bonuses together, and then it is passed from the highest level down through lower levels — each level taking money out of the pool for their group. Software developers are typically at the bottom of the pile. So that means that if bonuses are going out, everyone above you in the organization has to get their share and there still be enough left over. How do companies decide what goes into the pool? Well, often it is based on the company's performance. If the company has a good quarter or year, money will go into the pool.

The bonus pool means that bonuses might be getting paid out, but it just isn't making its way down to you.

Remember when I said that your bonus is described as a percentage of your salary? Well, that is your maximum bonus. Your minimum is zero. If a bonus does get paid out to you, it will never be more than your maximum, but it can easily be less than that.

Also, the conditions of receiving your bonus may be conditional on company performance, your team's performance, or your performance. I've never met a company that would give more clear criteria as to what any of those things mean. The lack of certainty around knowing if I'm in the running for a bonus means that I treat it as a coin flip.

Often when I realize that bonuses are a part of the compensation, I ask, "When was the last bonus paid?" The answer to that question will tell me how real the bonus is. If they haven't paid a bonus in a few years, I won't pay much attention to it. If they pay every year, I'll get excited. I highly recommend that you do not consider your bonus as money that you will earn or make when you are budgeting. Don't bet your mortgage or rent on a bonus.

Since bonuses are often described as a percentage of your salary, then the higher your salary, the higher your potential bonus. This relationship between bonus and salary greatly incentivizes the savvy interviewer to negotiate a higher salary, back to the hundred-thousand salary example. If you negotiate up to one-hundred and ten thousand dollars, then you just earned another ten thousand from salary. Negotiating that extra ten thousand gives you twenty-one thousand each year — ten from negotiating, and eleven thousand from the bonus.

Stock and Equity

Another common part of a compensation package and offer is stock or equity. This topic is fairly confusing, so I'll try only to cover the basics involved.

Essentially these two items boil down to the amount of the company you have. Employers offer stock to you as an option to purchase or in shares just like you can buy in the market. Only a company gives them to you with the "Option" to buy them at a price independent of the market. Equity is essentially the same, but exists privately within the company and conveys ownership.

Stock and equity come down to you being able to make money if the company grows and improves, and you are able to share your stock or equity in the company at the right time.

Vesting

If that isn't strange enough, stock, equity, and retirement often come with a vesting schedule. Vesting is essentially a time you have to wait until it's yours to use.

So for example, if you are going to get six hundred shares of stock vested over four years, you won't be able to use that stock until you've been at the company for four years.

Depending on the vesting terms, quitting early may mean you forfeit everything or some fraction of what you've accumulated through the vesting schedule. Looking at the vesting schedule helps you see when all that compensation they list in your package will actually be yours. Also, looking at the vesting schedule can help you make sense of where this particular job sits in terms of your career.

I recently quit a company before the vesting of my 401k was complete. That means I lost a significant portion of what the company contributed to my retirement. I calculated my loss from leaving the company and put that number next to a job that gets me further in my career. When I looked at the money that way, I was able to decide if I should stay or go.

Vacation and Sick Leave

If you're passionate about travel, seeing the world, or spending time with your family, vacation may be very important to you as a part of your compensation package.

In the software industry, it is common to start with somewhere between fifteen and twenty days paid vacation. You may or may not get sick days as well, and they may or may not roll over from year to year.

Companies have a lot of variety in how they give vacation. Sometimes it is one lump amount that includes sick leave and time off.

Sometimes they are separate. Pay attention to how they are listed. You will also want to consider the paid holidays they offer. If you need a set of holidays for your religious or other needs, now is the time to bring that up.

A footnote about vacation is that the more time they give to employees, the more liability the company has. Companies keep the money they are going to pay you while you're on vacation, off to the side. That pool of money represents a significant, unusable amount of cash that the company cannot use for anything. The overhead companies keep by giving vacation has given rise to them using some creative strategies.

Unlimited vacation is an approach companies can use to reduce their liability. If this is their policy, ask how you get to take a vacation. Sometimes it is unlimited, but "With manager approval only." In a job where you have a bad manager, this could mean you don't get any vacation and are made to feel guilty for being sick as well.

You may also want to ask if they have a standard vacation policy, how that vacation accrues, and if you can spend into debt if you join the company late in the year. The situation comes up often that you join a company but have a week of vacation planned. You won't have accrued the time off yet, so you need to spend the vacation time you'll earn later in the year. It's a pain to keep track of, but if they allow it, you have flexibility. If they don't, get used to taking big vacations at the end of the year.

Health Care

Healthcare is a complex subject. The essential parts are that you want access to healthcare, and you want your company to pay for as much of it as possible.

There are broadly two types of healthcare plans that you'll encounter, Preferred Provider Organization (PPO) and High-Deductible

Plan (HDP). Knowing the difference helps when you look at a company.

PPO plans tend to be more expensive every month for your premium, but your costs when you need care are lower. So you may pay more every month, but when you go to the doctor, it costs maybe twenty dollars. If you go to the hospital, many of the services will be covered. So you are trading a higher month-to-month with a lower incident cost.

HDP plans, on the other hand, have a lower monthly premium, but you have to deal with a higher deductible. You can almost think of it as the opposite of a PPO plan. The deductible component is how much you need to spend on healthcare beyond your monthly premium before your insurance helps. So if you have a three thousand dollar deductible, you will need to spend three thousand in health care before insurance helps. To offset these plans, they usually come with a Health-Savings Account (HSA). This is a bank account that you can put money into for health care.

While explaining all the details of how this works, and how to run scenarios, and pick the right plan is outside the scope of this book, knowing what kind of options you have is important at this moment. If they offer healthcare plans that are too expensive or don't meet your current or future medical needs, you need to know that now.

Think about if you'll be covering your family, starting a family, growing your family. If you have any health issues that require frequent or expensive treatment, weigh that as well. Health care is one of the biggest concerns for job-hunters. Many will stay in jobs they hate because the health care is excellent.

Retirement

Moving on to retirement, you want to look for a few things. First that they offer a 401k and that they match. Beyond that, it comes down to you and how you are planning to build wealth to ensure you make the most of the retirement offerings.

A 401k is an investment account. You use it to invest in the stock market. The unique part is that it comes with specific tax rules that are beneficial for employees investing for retirement. There are also rules if you take your money out before retirement. So, leveraging a 401k throughout your career offers you a unique way of preparing for retirement while managing your taxes along the way.

The matching that comes with your 401k is a perk many companies offer. Companies will offer to match dollar-to-dollar what you put into your account. If they provide a six percent match, they'll put in six percent of what you put in. They may set a maximum amount on it, or some other odd terms, but they all boil down to this basic concept.

What this means to you is that this perk offers you the chance to get a lot of extra money towards retirement for half the effort and cost. If you can afford to do it, I recommend that you minimally contribute up to your match. That way you get the free money from your company.

While many companies offer retirement, comparing their match is a way to separate companies along their benefits packages. Knowing this information helps you select companies to apply to as well as plan your financial future while employed.

Other Paperwork

Your package will contain numerous pages of legal documentation for you to sign. Often you'll see these papers after you've signed the offer. I do want to raise awareness of a few pieces that exist in almost every bit of hiring paperwork.

Your human resources folks can help you understand these pieces.

Non-Disclosure Agreement

These agreements are pretty standard. Read yours to see exactly what yours entails. The basics are that these agreements ask you never to share company secrets with people outside of the company. It is simple enough in principle, but it can be hard to know what constitutes a secret. For example, if you were part of some interesting internal project where you got really good at high-scale financial transactions, you'd also be a great candidate for another job. What part of the skills and knowledge that you developed are secrets, and which aren't?

My rule of thumb here is that I tend to avoid talking about any detail that was directly related to a company generating revenue. So in this example, the scalable transactions aren't the secret. The magic algorithm or business model that leveraged that scale is the secret.

Look at your NDA, note the terms, and if there are any expirations or if it exists forever. If your job is at an agency or consultancy where you'll have clients, have a conversation about how the NDA works.

Non-Compete, Non-Solicitation, and Moonlighting

These clauses in your paperwork all represent different aspects of employment beyond your job. While rarely do these clauses create any issues, they sometimes present a couple of challenges for the ambitious and opportunistic employee.

Non-compete clauses refer to preventing you from going straight over to your competitor. This clause relates to the NDA above. Many companies with a sales group will have non-compete terms in their employment packages. This clause exists to prevent some-one with a deep network of clients or leads taking them when they go to a competitor. For software development, it is unlikely to cause an issue unless you work for a consultancy or agency.

Non-solicitation is a bit trickier to understand. This clause exists to prevent poaching employees. The idea is that if you leave, you can't come back and try to get current employees to work with you somewhere else. This policy also applies to the reverse scenario as well. If there are consultants at your job, you cannot solicit them to work with you either. For many developers, this won't be an issue but talk with your managers and human resources people to better understand how this works.

As you work in the field, you'll build a network of people you trust and want to work with. Understanding how non-solicitation clauses work helps you work with these people regularly throughout your career.

Lastly, we have moonlighting. Moonlighting is when you take or have a side-job. You may teach or mentor in your free time. You may be involved with open-source. You may be building a video game. Most of the time, your company won't care unless it competes with them. It is still a good idea to bring up their policy and the clause and mention what you want to or do work on so it can be written in as an exclusion.

Related to moonlighting, there are sometimes clauses that exist that attempt to give ownership of your work to the company. Moonlighting is only one of the places where that can happen.

Intellectual Property

Somewhere in your hiring packet, there will be a section that will go over intellectual property rights. I want you to pay very close attention to it.

At a minimum, these clauses will say that anything you do with company equipment or time is the property of the company. This minimum clause comes with several implications that very few companies think through. If you work for a company and they want you to sign this document but work on your personal computer, stop. As soon as you agree to use your personal computer for work, you have also transferred everything you've done to the company as well. Every side project is their property. Every good idea in an email is theirs.

It is sometimes hard to set such clear boundaries, but start the conversation. In the HBO series Silicon Valley, they bring this situation up as the main character who built a side project gets taken to court by his employer. They attempted to prove that he violated these clauses by using company time or equipment on his side project. The situation resolved when it was revealed that the employment contracts were all illegal and unenforceable.

While this show is a parody, it is well-researched. Many parts of this section and your offer paperwork may be unenforceable or even illegal. Reading your paperwork gives you an idea of what they are asking of you. If it seems unreasonable, say something.

Now, I mentioned the minimum clauses claim everything you do with their time or equipment belongs to the company. They can sometimes go beyond by claiming everything you do while employed belongs to them. I do not sign these agreements. Human resources will always assure me that it doesn't mean anything, but I refuse. Remember, these clauses transfer ownership to the company. I always have side-projects I'm tinkering with, and I'm not giving them all away for free.

If you see that more expansive version, bring it up. Making sure you know what you are signing helps you understand the boundaries between your job and personal life and ambitions. Ambitious developers have built so many great things in their free time. If you have a great idea, pursue it, and make sure the company's participation in it is clearly defined.

Negotiation

Now that the boring stuff is out of the way, let's talk about how to negotiate better compensation. Be warned, attempting this takes a fantastic amount of courage. If the interview process was stressful, get ready.

Before I jump into the details of how I negotiate, I want to make a note for the first-time job-hunters. I typically don't advocate you negotiate your first job. The reasons are that you are unlikely to have a wealth of experience behind you to justify how amazing you are, and you have to be able to walk away. First-timers rarely fit those two criteria. I recommend instead that you get the first job, and start negotiating your second job.

There are a few things throughout the book I've mentioned about negotiation, and there are a few principals I'll bring up:

- First one to say a number loses
- Always 10% more
- Have a reason
- Be prepared to walk away
- It isn't just salary

First One to Say a Number Loses

Throughout your interview process, interviewers will ask what your salary history is, or what you want to make. If you're going to set yourself up to negotiate well, avoid those questions.

I respond to those requests by saying something like, "I'm more interested in seeing if we're a good fit. If we are, I'm confident we'll find a number that works."

If you work with recruiters, it can be a bit more difficult as they don't usually like negotiation and will want to set a number very early in the process. At this later stage in my career, I prohibit recruiters from discussing compensation on my behalf.

Now, let's say you do speak a number at some point in the process. All hope isn't lost; it's just less ideal. When you offer a number, the company will check against the salary bands they have in place. If you said something too high or too low, it might not go well for you. You are unlikely to know the band, so you'll be guessing based on your sense of worth and the market. However, from the moment that number comes out, that number will anchor the rest of your compensation discussion. If you anchored to a low part of the salary band, that is the compensation you will negotiate.

When they have to give a number they are forced to weigh a few things. First, they will pick a number within their band. Second, they have to decide if they want to go back to interviewing again, and third, the company has to decide how badly they want you now. Most companies are fatigued by interviewing, and when they find someone, they want to hire them. These factors tend to encourage a higher number when they offer one first.

Always 10% More

So if you're going to negotiate, how much should you ask for? Well, I recommend you start by asking for ten percent more than your offer. If they offer one hundred thousand, ask for one hundred and ten thousand.

Now, this is a simple guideline, but it works almost every time. Feel free to change the number to whatever you think is right. If you know your value and the market demand is way higher than ten percent, you ask for what you are worth and what the market supports.

The reason ten percent works well is that by the time you are negotiating, the company has spent a lot of time, energy, and money finding you. When a company hires you, they also pay their parts of the benefits, equipment, adjustments to their insurance, and so on. Their total cost having you employed is significant, but ten percent doesn't feel that way. Also, asking for ten percent for this process to be over feels like a cheap purchase.

If you're unsure where to start, start by asking for ten percent more than the offer.

Have a Reason

When you get the offer, you'll likely be talking with human resources. They are unable to negotiate with you most of the time. So when you negotiate, they'll have to take it back to the managers for approval. Providing a reason helps them present your case adequately and give you the best chance. Without providing a reason, they can look at you compared to a similar candidate who didn't ask.

You want to have a list of things about you that are incredible that may not have come out in your interview. Throughout your various jobs, I recommend you create a notebook where you can jot down incredible feedback you get, and your accomplishments. The interview process will pull some of the juicier bits out, but if you do this simple practice, you'll have dozens or hundreds of examples to justify higher compensation.

You don't need to worry if your list of things equals the amount you're negotiating for. You only need to sell it. Just like when writing a resume, you write for the outcomes and impacts, you talk about the outcomes and impacts you have here too. This practice also prepares you for a raise while employed.

When you look at the compensation package, you may also notice certain holes or issues that are good reasons to negotiate with as well. I joined one company and negotiated an extra ten percent because their healthcare was inadequate. Another, I negotiated the amount of my bonus because they hadn't paid them regularly. I kept the bonus as well.

Whether your history is full of gems, or the compensation package itself offers the opportunity, have a reason you use when negotiating.

Be Prepared to Walk Away

When you negotiate, you are asking for something that they can refuse. You need to be prepared to hear the rejection of your negotiation mentally. You have to be mentally prepared to walk away.

Now, you may not walk away, but if your frame of mind is there, you can negotiate confidently. You can also look at the situation from a place of confidence instead of desperation. That confidence will help you see the company as one you can choose to work with instead of one that you need to work for.

This attitude is a reason I typically recommend first-timers avoiding negotiation. Many are trying so desperately to break into the industry that the thought of losing the job over negotiation is too much. Don't negotiate that first time if that's you. Take the job. Know this isn't your forever job, and you can try again in a few months.

It Isn't Just the Salary

Salary may be the most obvious thing to negotiate, but it is far from the only thing. Here's a list of other parts of your compensation you may want to think about:

- Bonus
- Stock

- Vacation
- Childcare
- Transportation
- Professional development
- Equipment
- Working hours
- Remote work

This list is far from exhaustive, but it does highlight that beyond the money you make, there are things you can negotiate. Part of knowing what to ask for is knowing what lifestyle you want. Once you can visualize the life you want to have, you know more clearly what you need from this job to get closer to it. If you have children and the stress of paying for childcare is taking the life out of you, see if the company will offset the costs. If you're in a major metropolitan area where traffic is terrible, or parking is awful, negotiate a transportation stipend so you aren't worried about getting to work. Negotiate a better life for yourself.

Signing the Offer

You passed the interviews, you've negotiated, and you have the final offer. You're ready to accept. There is one last detail I must bring up before we are all done, and you can enjoy this moment.

Many people have a hard time knowing when to talk about interviewing, the potential or received offer, or providing notice to their current job. With good reason, it is confusing, and it feels like if you make a mistake here, things can go south.

The rule of thumb I advocate you follow is that you don't say anything to anyone until you have a signed offer. Everything can change until you've put a pen to that paper. Verbal offers can be rescinded. The job can vanish during negotiation. It isn't until you accept the offer in writing that you have a job.

The harm in talking about interviewing or potential offers you have is that your current employer will likely have to make plans to transition you out of your current responsibilities. They will do this before you provide notice. That means that you could wind up sitting at your current job with nothing to do, and if your new job falls through, you'll be in a tough position. By this time, others are doing your work, the company is expecting you to quit, and yet you remain. More often than not, this situation feels so awkward that many developers leave. The downside is they don't have a job lined up.

Say nothing until the offer is signed.

When you do sign the offer, the next bit is submitting your notice. Depending on where you live and the local laws, you may have to provide a certain amount of notice to your employer. Do your homework. If you live in an at-will state, you can quit at any moment without any reason and without penalty. Knowing the laws regarding terminating your employment are important, as they change how you may leave.

It is pretty common to provide two weeks of notice. Giving notice means that you go to your boss with a written resignation indicating that your last day will be two weeks from when you submit the resignation. This event triggers your transfer of responsibilities, and human resources will begin to arrange the termination of your benefits. Even if you are in a job you hate, I don't recommend quitting in a flashy way that gives you personal satisfaction at the expense of others.

We live in a surprisingly small world, and word travels quickly. If a story about you travels far enough, you may find that a future employer knows that you are a jerk when you quit, and they may decide to pass on you before you ever have a shot. Leave on professional terms. Be clear about your last day, and take it upon yourself to transition your knowledge and responsibilities to a new person.

11 - We've Landed

First, I want to thank you for reading *Land the Job*! If you've read this far, you have everything you need to get your first software job and change jobs as often as you like to create the career and lifestyle you've always wanted.

As in all things worth having, my approach requires discipline and focus, and at times flies in the face of a lot of other advice people are giving.

Years ago, I was on the fence about taking a job in the government where I'd have stability and no passion or going for a more dynamic company with way more risk, but that I had more passion for. I wasn't sure what to do, so I asked a friend. He said that I should think about the lifestyle I want more than the job. Then, take the job that gets me a step closer. After all, it's a job, not my entire life.

That conversation, together with a lot of thought and research, has led me to the approach and techniques I wrote here. I started seeing jobs as a means to the life I want instead of a destination in itself. That subtle shift caused me to think about the nature of getting the right job, and then turning that job into the opportunity I want. I refined my craft, taught and mentored others, and wrote this book.

I hope you've found it helpful, and through its application, you find a more fulfilling life and career.

What is Next For You?

This book covers what is needed to land a job in software quickly. That's a skill you can develop and apply whenever you want. Where does this skill live in your idea of your career and life? What does this current job do to add to your life? What are you experiencing here in this job that will be a great story the next time you're interviewing?

The act of choosing to get a new job takes place because something else in your life or career isn't fulfilling enough. Keep going, reaching, and growing.

Everyone asks in an interview, "Where do you see yourself in the next five years?" I've found that very few people are prepared for a real answer. Shock them with your clarity of purpose. Tell them exactly why this job matters, why you are precisely in the right place at the right time for them and you.

Develop your stories, make time to reflect. Keep those resumes, portfolios, and everything else up-to-date. You'll always be ready for the next opportunity by checking back in with where you are every few months.

It may seem ridiculous, but you and everyone else who learns the skill of getting the job they want will have a massive impact on the industry. The thought that many organizations cling to, "They're lucky to be here," will change to, "We're lucky to have them." When the workforce effortlessly walks away from inadequate companies and their cultures, those companies will have to evolve or die.

Your ability to remain utterly fluid in the market and your peers' ability to do so can be a powerful catalyst for companies to improve.

Keep In Touch

I wasn't ordained by anyone to write this book or offer my advice. I just decided to put this out there. I'm just a guy figuring out his life like everyone else.

I want to know what you think. I want to hear your questions. I want to keep helping. Reach out to me!

Tell me how this book helped!